THE MICROWAVE

FRENCH COOKBOOK

THELMA SNYDER and MARCIA CONE

PRENTICE HALL PRESS
New York London Toronto Sydney Tokyo

Microwave ovens cook food differently than standard ovens. In order to prepare the recipes in this book safely and successfully, follow precisely the directions given.

Published in 1988 by Prentice Hall Press
A Division of Simon & Schuster, Inc.
Gulf + Western Building
One Gulf + Western Plaza
New York, NY 10023

Originally published in 1983 by Van Nostrand Reinhold Company, Inc.

PRENTICE HALL PRESS is a registered trademark of Simon & Schuster, Inc.

Library of Congress Cataloging-in-Publication Data

Snyder, Thelma.
    The microwave French cookbook / Thelma Snyder and Marcia Cone.—
1st Prentice Hall Press ed.
        p.   cm.
    Reprint. Originally published: New York: Van Nostrand Reinhold,
© 1983.
    Includes index.
    ISBN 0-13-582123-1
    1. Cookery, French. 2. Microwave cookery. I. Cone, Marcia.
II. Title.
[TX719.S588   1988]   87-28421   641.5′882—dc19

Designed by Norma Levarie

Photographs by David Arky

Wines furnished courtesy of
Sherry-Lehman Inc., 679 Madison
Avenue, New York, and Dreadnought
Wines, 9425 Stenton Avenue,
Philadelphia.

Manufactured in the United States of America

10 9 8 7 6 5 4 3 2 1

First Prentice Hall Press Edition

CONTENTS

ACKNOWLEDGMENTS

Thanks to Dave for taking charge of the household during those long photography sessions in New York, and to the kids for sacrificing fries at McDonald's for months of leftover French food. To the Cones for hours of proofing in which we pondered monumental questions, such as, should "dough side up" be hyphenated? We gave it a thumb side down.

To Susan Cioni and Marge Keren for their excellent taste in china and silver. Each piece was a picture in itself before it ever found its way into ours. To photographer David Arky, for the special attention he gave to each picture. And to Charles F. Lamalle, importers of French dishware, 1123 Broadway, New York.

To modern technology, Chuck Schroth and the TRS-80 Model 1. And to Jöel Assouline for being our sounding board.

INTRODUCTION

"The Microwave French Cookbook." Maybe you are thinking that this is just another book to get buried beneath the cookie cutters and Grandpa's bottle of medicinal sherry. But we feel it will be the means to catapult you into a whole new style of cooking, and the result will be a host of inventive dishes that you can claim as your own.

If we told you that with the aid of this book, and your microwave, you would be able to whip up a Chocolate-Mocha Mousse in fifteen minutes, or a foolproof Orange Hollandaise Sauce in five to ten, would you be interested? What would you think if we told you this book would teach you a new technique for making a tart shell from a melt-in-your mouth butter pastry called a Pâte Brisée? And does the thought of a chocolate cake with chocolate filling, chocolate icing, and chocolate glaze cause you to salivate uncontrollably? If so, you are a candidate for our Gâteau au Chocolat.

When you cook *à la mode de chez nous,* as the French would say, or "our way," nothing but fresh herbs and ingredients will do. We follow suit and call for them as an essential part of our recipes. Stock bases are important, too, and we've given you methods for making your own beef and chicken stocks in much less time than it would take to do them conventionally. (The trick is to make a large amount of stock once in a great while, then freeze it in ice-cube trays to be reconstituted easily later.)

You will find selections from the classics such as Boeuf Bourguignon, Soupe à l'Oignon, and Steak au Poivre, flambéed in the microwave. We have captured treasures from some of the many imaginative regional cuisines of France, including Clafouti

Limousin, a custard tart with cherries from Limousin, Jambon Braisé à la Normande, a braised ham with apples and cream, Normandy style, and Bourride, the lemon-colored fish soup bearing the distinctive stamp of Provence—garlic.

Why should such pleasures as these be left to the chefs, or the people with time and copper pots? As a French chef once said, "To know how to cook is to love cooking." Now you have a new way to cook: French cooking in the microwave.

1

Guide for Successful French Cooking: Microwave Techniques, Utensils, Ingredients

TERMS USED IN RECIPES

Arranging foods with the thicker sections toward the outside permits more even cooking. This is because most of the microwave energy is received by the foods on the outer edges of the dish.

Cooking powers designated in the recipes will be one of these four, which are based on a standard 600–700 watt oven:

High	(100%)
Reheat	(80%)
Medium	(50%)
Low	(10%)

Foods that benefit from lower power settings are those with more delicate ingredients such as sauces, and those incorporating eggs or cheese. Less tender cuts of meat also need lower power settings to lengthen cooking time for tenderization and development of flavors.

Once the power is listed in the recipe it remains the same throughout the recipe, unless otherwise stated. Powers will be italicized if we feel the power change to a lower one might be overlooked.

Cooking times can vary with oven wattage or the electrical power output in the home. Use the shortest cooking times given, then cook longer if necessary.

Cover with lid or vented plastic wrap means to cover with a dish lid or, when no lid is available, plastic wrap that is folded back slightly on one corner to allow some heat and steam to escape. The dish lid does not need to be vented because the steam that builds up will lift the lid slightly and escape as it would with the vented wrap.

Covering in this manner keeps the food moist and shortens the cooking time.

Cover loosely with wax paper means to lay a piece of wax paper on top of the dish to prevent spatters and speed cooking in foods that do not need steaming for tenderizing.

Cover with paper towel to absorb excess moisture while allowing steam to escape, as when cooking fish.

If no cover is mentioned, the food is cooked uncovered.

Cover with foil to protect larger bone areas from overcooking, as in the recipe for Leg of Lamb with Parsley Crumbs. Wrap foil smoothly and tightly as directed, so that no rough edges protrude. Foil can be used on the ends of large pieces of meat also, if they appear to be cooking too quickly.

Doubling of recipes is possible. Use the same procedure and power setting of the original recipe, but rather than doubling cooking time, add half again as much time to equal one-and-one-half the time of the original recipe.

Preparation time is an estimate of total preparation time from the raw ingredient to the finished product i.e., chopping, cooking, standing time, and chilling. As your proficiency with each recipe increases, the preparation time will decrease.

Rearranging dishes placed in a circular pattern in the oven means moving the dishes from front to back or side to side, depending on the cooking pattern of the oven.

Note: Microwave cooking is not heat convection, in fact it involves *no* internal heat in the oven. The foods are cooked by high frequency radio waves that activate the food molecules at the same speed (or number of cycles) as the radio waves, in this case 2½ million times per second. As the food molecules are vibrated, they begin to generate heat within the food. The microwaves penetrate the food ½ to ¾ of an inch from the outside edges; the interior of the food is cooked by heat conduction.

Because there are between 30 and 40 manufacturers of microwave ovens offering 2 or 3 different models each, there are many different ways in which the microwave energy can be distributed within the ovens. The energy distribution is called the "cooking pattern" and to compensate for this variable, it is necessary to reposition and rotate food during cooking.

Repositioning food within the dish insures even cooking. As the food cooks, the highest concentration of energy is along the outside edge of the dish, so foods should be positioned with the thicker portions to the outside. Foods that cannot be stirred, such as chicken legs, are repositioned to move those outside pieces to the inside, and vice versa, to equalize the cooking times of each piece.

Note: This can be done inside or outside the oven because there is no heat generated in the oven, hence no chance to burn oneself. Every oven owner learns this the first time he or she reheats coffee right in the cup, and is able to reach in and take it out by the handle.

Rotating or turning a dish clockwise is sometimes done with foods that cannot be stirred, repositioned, or turned over. Rotating will mean either one half, one third, or one quarter turn as indicated by the recipe. Depending on your oven's cooking pattern, you may need less rotation, or none at all.

A food sensor is an accessory instrument included in some, but not all, microwave ovens. It consists of a temperature probe, a plug, and an oven receptacle. A food sensor aids in determining the doneness of food by turning the oven off when a prescribed temperature has been reached. Ovens with food sensors include instructions for operation.

Standing time allows foods to finish cooking by heat conduction. (Heat is built up by the rapid movement of food molecules during cooking.) Unless otherwise stated, foods should stand on a flat surface (not a cooling rack) to allow the internal heat to work in the food, rather than be allowed to cool off by the surrounding air. Denser foods, like meat, will stand for 10 minutes. During this time the internal temperature will rise 10° to 15°F. Less dense foods, like vegetables or eggs, will stand for 1 to 5 minutes.

Turning over is necessary, part way through cooking, for recipes that call for large pieces of meat like leg of lamb, ham, or beef roast.

Preparing accompaniments (vegetables, sauces, rice, etc.):

do this during the standing time of a main dish. Most vegetables will take no more than 10 minutes to cook, which will fit into this time slot. Sauces are quickly prepared and can be cooked during standing time, or can be prepared earlier to be reheated right before serving. Rice, although it can be cooked in the microwave, is better cooked on top of the stove to allow the microwave to be used for other dishes.

MENU PLANNING
Hors d'oeuvres and desserts can be prepared earlier in the day, and many of their flavors will improve with time and/or refrigeration.

UTENSILS
Browning dishes have been treated with a special material that absorbs microwave energy. When preheated in the microwave, the center area rises in temperature to between 200° and 600°F. This enables foods to be seared and browned, while being cooked for a short period of time.

Browning dishes come in various sizes and are in either the grill type—a flat dish with a well to catch juices—or a casserole with sides and a lid.

A *casserole* is a round or oval dish at least 3 inches deep which may have its own lid. When a food is being brought to a boil, the food should only half fill the casserole to avoid the possibility of boiling over. Because liquids heat so quickly in the microwave, they tend to boil up more quickly and higher than on a stove top.

The classic French casserole, which is oval in shape, is perfect for microwave cooking because it has no corners where microwave energy can build up to overcook foods.

A *custard cup* is a small glass or ceramic dish with about 6-ounce capacity.

A *flat dish*, with dimensions given, is called for when foods need to be arranged in one layer to cook evenly and quickly. Pie or cake plates can be used here if they are large enough to hold the volume of food.

A *food processor* or blender can save preparation time in recipes calling for chopping, grinding, or mixing.

A *grapefruit knife* facilitates the coring of pears and removing the fruit from pineapple shells.

A long-bladed metal spatula will aid in the unmolding and icing of certain desserts, and in making decorative chocolate triangles.

A microwave dish means a glass or ceramic dish that transfers microwave energy to the food. It should not have any metal trim and should be able to withstand heat up to 400°F.

A microwave muffin pan is a 6- to 12-cup plastic muffin pan used to cook individual muffins or biscuits. In these recipes we ask you to turn it over to form individual tart shells.

Glass measures holding 1 cup and 4 cups are called for often. We find them handy utensils to use for measuring, cooking, and pouring.

Ramekins or *ramequins* are small porcelain or glass casseroles with about 6-ounce capacity. They are different from custard cups in being straight-sided and shallower.

A roasting rack is a utensil of ceramic, tempered plastic, or paper, that enables meat to be raised above the dish in which it cooks. This prevents overcooking of the underside of the meat or steaming of foods where a drier crust is desired.

A simmerpot is a porous clay pot that is soaked in cold water before cooking to aid in the tenderization of tough cuts of meat.

A simmerpot adaptable to the microwave is one with a glazed interior on the bottom half. During cooking, the moisture soaked into the pot is released to tenderize meats and blend flavors. If you use a clay pot without a glazed bottom, the cooking times will be slightly longer.

The simmerpot is the preferred cooking method when called for, but it is not necessary to the success of the recipe.

A wire whisk is important for stirring sauces.

INGREDIENTS

Good recipes deserve high-quality fresh foods for the best results. Here are some specific ingredients we find critical to success.

Beef stock or chicken stock should be made according to the recipe given, or purchased in the can. Avoid beef or chicken cubes, which will add too much salt to the recipe.

Butter that is unsalted is preferred for flavor and texture, especially in pastries and desserts. Margarine can be substituted for butter in all recipes.

Cheese is often served on a dessert plate with fruit. It should be served at room temperature. Bring ½ pound refrigerated cheese to room temperature by heating on Medium (50% power) for 45 seconds to 1 minute, depending on density of cheese.

Eggs should be large. We have listed this specifically in the Eggs, Cakes and Pastries, and Desserts chapters where we feel it is most critical to the recipe.

Herbs should be fresh whenever available, but we have given dried alternatives. When you have an abundance of fresh herbs, chop them up and freeze in moistureproof containers for later use. The best way to reduce a bay leaf to pieces is to crush it with your fingertips. Fennel seeds must be crushed with the back of a spoon, a wide knife blade, or mortar and pestle.

Lemon juice should be fresh; it is far superior to bottled or canned juice. To get more juice from your lemons, place one or two lemons in the microwave on Low (10% power) for 1 minute.

Lemon or orange rind is only the colored outer part of the peel, not including any of the bitter white portion.

Tomatoes peel easily when plunged into boiling water. Put water in a microwave casserole, enough to cover the number of tomatoes that need to be peeled. Cover with a lid or vented plastic wrap, to speed boiling, and heat the water on High until it comes to a boil. Remove the bowl from the oven and plunge each tomato into the hot water for a few seconds. Remove tomatoes and peel.

Wines and liqueurs are used to impart special flavors to many dishes, from appetizers to desserts. Notice, we said flavor and not alcoholic content because the alcohol evaporates during cooking. The wine you cook with should be something drinkable, not those labeled "cooking wines." All of the liqueurs listed in recipes for flaming are at least 80 proof. Any substitutes should be at least 80 proof, also, in order for them to ignite.

MEASUREMENTS AND EQUIVALENTS
VOLUMES

		QUART	PINT	FLUID OUNCES	CUPS	TABLE- SPOONS	TEA- SPOONS	MILLI- LITER (ml)	DROPS
1 quart	=	2		32	4			946	
1 cup	=		½	8		16		237	
½ cup	=			4		8		118	
¼ cup	=			2		4		59	
⅛ cup	=			1		2		30	
1 tablespoon	=			½			3	15	
1 teaspoon	=			⅙		⅓		5	
½ teaspoon	=							2.5	
¼ teaspoon	=							1.2	
1 dash	=								2 to 4

WEIGHTS

		OUNCES BY WEIGHT	GRAMS (g)	GRAINS
1 pound	=	16	454	
½ pound	=	8	227	
¼ pound	=	4	113	
⅛ pound	=	2	56	
1 ounce	=		28	
½ ounce	=		14	
1 pinch	=			a few

2

Les Hors-d'Oeuvre

Appetizers

Just because the hors d'oeuvre began as something that meant "outside the chef's main job," the choice of it should not be left until you are passing through the "crackers and snacks" aisle in the grocery store. Often decided after the main dish, vegetable, and dessert have been chosen, this course still holds a key position in the scheme of meal planning.

An hors d'oeuvre is designed to refresh, titillate, and prepare the palate for the foods to come. It should always be in harmony with the rest of the meal and should put your guests in good spirits along with any other spirits you serve. Even though an appetizer shouldn't overpower the meal, it can keep the portion of the meat or expensive main course to a minimum, for it tends to take up some of the appetite slack. On all of these points we are in agreement with the French about the attributes of appetizers; we differ when it comes to how the hors d'oeuvre should be served.

On the continent, an hors d'oeuvre is presented at the table, to be eaten with a knife and fork. In this country we often start a meal with tidbits that can be eaten with fingers, while we are mingling with guests over cocktails. The recipes in this chapter are adaptable to either situation. The salads like Légumes à la Grecque (Greek-style marinated vegetables) or Salade de Pommes de Terre au Vin Blanc (potato salad with white wine) are easier to navigate with a knife and fork at the table. But we'll let you be the judge as to whether the Terrine de Maison (chilled meat terrine with nuts) or Tartelettes aux Champignons (mushroom tarts) are better eaten with flatware or your fingers.

Pâté de Foie de Volaille

Chicken Liver Pâté

Pâté de foie gras with truffles might be what you would order in an elegant French restaurant, but as for preparation at home, who can find goose livers, and who can afford truffles? Here we have a cheaper but just as delicious version; even non-pâté lovers go for it! The more astute of you may see that we are trying to pass off black olives as truffles. We never thought you would be fooled, but a quick glance at your hors d'oeuvre table will give that "money-is-no-object" appearance. Remember that the French are known for their charades, too.

Servings: 8 to 10   Preparation time: 30 minutes
                                             plus 6 hours to
                                             chill

2 pieces bacon, diced
1 tablespoon chopped shallot, or sliced green onion
1 teaspoon minced garlic
1 pound chicken livers
¼ pound butter, softened
2 tablespoons Cognac or brandy
2 tablespoons chopped parsley
1 teaspoon chopped fresh gingerroot, or ½ teaspoon ground
    ginger
½ teaspoon dry mustard
½ teaspoon dried thyme
½ teaspoon salt, or to taste
¼ teaspoon marjoram
4 black olives, chopped
Chopped whole hard-cooked egg for garnish

In a 2-quart microwave casserole, combine bacon, shallot, and garlic. Cook on High for 2 minutes, or until shallot pieces are softened.

Add chicken livers and cover with lid or vented plastic wrap. Cook on *Medium* (50% power) for 10 minutes, or until thoroughly cooked, stirring halfway through. Remove from oven and allow to stand covered for 5 minutes.

Put a few spoonfuls of liver mixture into blender or food processor and grind until fine. Transfer to a separate bowl. Add a few more spoonfuls to blender and grind. Continue to process until all the liver mixture is ground. Add remaining ingredients except hard-cooked egg, and stir. Pack into a 3-cup crock and chill thoroughly, about 6 hours.

Garnish with chopped egg and serve with Melba toast or thin slices of toasted French bread.

Serve with a Bordeaux-Graves or Beaujolais.

VARIATION

Pâté en Croûte can be made by stuffing a long loaf of French bread with the pâté mixture. Cut the ends from a loaf of French bread, then cut the loaf, crosswise into halves. With a wooden spoon handle, push the bread through to hollow out center of each half to within ½ inch of crust. Spoon chilled pâté into the hollows; wrap in foil, and chill. Remove foil and serve by slicing loaf into ½-inch slices.

TIPS

The butter can be softened on Low (10% power) for 30 seconds.

Chicken livers are cooked on Medium so they will not pop. Chicken livers, mushrooms, and eggs out of the shell have membranes that burst because of the quick heat buildup if cooked on a higher power.

Terrine de Maison

Chilled Meat Terrine with Nuts

Pâté in French is the name of the meat paste, but it is also used for the meat mixture baked in a pastry crust, to be served either hot or cold. (This kind of pâté is also called *pâté en croûte*.) A "terrine" is a ground meat mixture named from the dish, the terrine, in which it is baked. The pastry lining is replaced by one of bacon (in France unsalted fresh pork fat), and a terrine is always served cold. Our version falls somewhere in between because it is served chilled but has neither a pastry nor bacon lining; thus we've called it "House Terrine."

Servings: 8 for first course
250 appetizers
on crackers

Preparation time: 30 to 40 minutes
plus 5 to 24
hours to cool

1 tablespoon butter
¼ cup finely chopped shallots
½ pound pork, ground
½ pound veal or turkey, ground
½ pound ham, ground
2 eggs, slightly beaten
½ cup coarsely chopped walnuts
2 tablespoons Cognac, vermouth, or sherry
½ teaspoon salt
¼ teaspoon ground allspice
¼ teaspoon freshly grated nutmeg
¼ teaspoon crushed thyme

In a 2-quart microwave or glass loaf dish (9 × 5 inches), combine butter and shallots. Cook on High for 1½ minutes, or until shallots are softened. Add remaining ingredients, mixing with hands or wooden spoon until well blended. Press evenly into the loaf dish. Cover loosely with wax paper and cook for 20 to 25 minutes on *Medium* (50% power), or until pâté reaches 155°F with food sensor, rotating twice during cooking. The terrine is done when the top is firm to the touch and the loaf shrinks slightly from the sides; the juices should run clear yellow instead of pink.

Remove from oven. Removing wax paper, but leaving terrine in pan, cover the top with foil. Place a 3- to 4-pound weight on top of the foil (a rock or brick will do as will several filled food or coffee cans) and cool to room temperature. Flavor improves if weighted and chilled overnight. To serve, remove weight and foil. Remove meat from dish and slice.

Serve with a Bordeaux-Médoc or Beaujolais.

TIPS

The weight on the terrine compresses it, making it a more solid mass and allowing for easier slicing.

The 155°F measured by the food sensor will rise to 170°F during standing time.

SERVING SUGGESTIONS

As a first course: Cut into ½-inch-thick slices and serve on a lettuce leaf with mustard and cornichons, or small gherkins.

As an appetizer: Spread a thin layer of Mayonnaise aux Fines Herbes (page 42) on Melba toast or crackers. Cut pâté into thin diamond shapes and arrange on the crackers spread with mayonnaise.

La Tentation de Bramafan

Eggplant Caviar

How can one really call an eggplant dish, a caviar? The texture is slightly beady, like caviar; the taste is surprisingly like fish but less salty. You may even find some of your friends preferring this imitation to the real thing. Serve it on crackers or as a vegetable dip.

Quantity: about 2 cups   Preparation time: 10 minutes
                                                   plus 30 minutes
                                                   to chill

1 medium-size eggplant
1 medium-size tomato, peeled, seeded, and finely chopped
1 medium-size onion, finely chopped
1 garlic clove, minced
3 tablespoons olive oil
2 tablespoons vinegar
1 teaspoon sugar
1 teaspoon chopped fresh gingerroot, or ¼ teaspoon ground
    ginger
½ teaspoon salt
¼ teaspoon freshly ground pepper

Prick whole eggplant in a few places with a stainless-steel fork and place on a paper towel or plate. Cook on High for 5 to 7 minutes, or until softened. Allow to cool in the refrigerator for about 30 minutes.

Cut eggplant lengthwise into halves and scoop out the inside flesh. Place the flesh in the bowl of a blender, food processor, or electric mixer. Process, blend, or mix until eggplant is puréed. Add remaining ingredients and mix well. Spoon into a bowl.

Keep chilled until ready to serve, then surround bowl with crackers or raw vegetables.

TIPS
By using the microwave to cook the eggplant you eliminate about 40 minutes of time that would be used for oven roasting.

For ease in peeling the tomato, see Ingredients, page 8.

Brie au Beurre et aux Amandes

Melted Brie with Butter and Almonds

Students in Paris eat many a dinner that consists of nothing more than cheese, bread, and wine. It is hardly a menu selected from all of the basic four food groups, but one compatible with the image of the struggling creative artist. Brie cheese was one of our favorites and had we been able to afford butter and almonds (Brie was already a luxury), we could have easily lived on this dish; it's delicious!

Servings: 8 to 10   Preparation time: 5 to 8 minutes

½ to 1 pound Brie cheese
3 tablespoons butter
¼ cup slivered almonds

Cut Brie horizontally into halves. Place each half, skin side down, on a separate serving platter and cut into 1-inch squares.

Place butter in a custard cup or 1-cup glass measure and cook on High for 45 seconds, or until melted. Pour over Brie and sprinkle with nuts. Cook cheese on Medium (50% power) for 3 to 5 minutes. (Cheese should be soft enough to dip into with crackers.)

Serve immediately with butter crackers or plain wafers.
Serve with a Bordeaux or Anjou Rouge.

VARIATION
Substitute chopped walnuts or hazelnuts for almonds.

Tartelettes aux Champignons

Mushroom Tarts

Servings: 6   Preparation time: 1½ hours
                                 including 1 hour to
                                 chill pastry dough

Pâte Brisée (Plain Pastry Dough, page 122)
1 medium-size onion, finely chopped
3 tablespoons butter
½ pound mushrooms, sliced, reserving 2 whole mushrooms for
    garnish
¼ cup chopped fresh parsley
2 tablespoons sherry, or dry vermouth
1 tablespoon lemon juice
1 tablespoon flour
½ teaspoon salt
¼ teaspoon freshly ground pepper

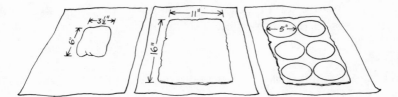

Prepare pastry dough and shape into a rectangle, 6 by 3½ inches before chilling.

Roll pastry into a rectangle, 16 by 11 inches; cut into six 5-inch circles. Use each to cover the reverse side of a muffin cup on a microwave muffin pan, pressing dough to edges; or use six 2½-inch ramekins or custard cups, pressing the dough up about 1½ inches on the sides. With tines of fork, press dough edges against sides of cups, and prick surfaces with fork every ½ inch or so.

Place inverted muffin pan or cups, dough side up, in the microwave. Cups should be arranged in a circular pattern, allowing 1-inch space between them. Cook on High for 5 to 6 minutes, or until dry and opaque (pastry will not brown), rotating pan one half turn and repositioning cups halfway through cooking. Remove from oven and allow crusts to cool.

Meanwhile, in a 1½-quart casserole, combine onion and butter. Cook on High for 2 minutes. Add remaining ingredients; mix well. Cook for 2 minutes; stir. Cook for 2 minutes more.

After crusts have cooled, gently remove them from cups and trim any uneven edges with scissors. Spoon mushroom mixture into tartlet shells, dividing evenly among the six. (At this point, tartlets can be refrigerated, to be reheated on High for 5 to 8 minutes.) Trim and slice 2 reserved mushrooms to garnish tarts.

Just before serving, reheat on High for 3 to 4 minutes, until hot (unless tartlets have been refrigerated).

TIPS
When arranging custard cups, do not forget the 1-inch space between them; it is important for even cooking.

When baking pastry shells, check for doneness a minute before the end of cooking time, since crusts will differ in thickness. Look for a dry, opaque appearance.

Timbales de Broccoli

Broccoli Timbales

These timbales are green-flecked custards with creamy interiors. Buttering and breading the custard dishes gives them a brown crust and makes them easy to unmold. A food processor will cut down preparation time considerably.

Servings: 6   Preparation time: 30 minutes
                              plus 5 minutes
                              to stand

3 tablespoons butter
¾ cup dry bread crumbs
2 cups peeled and finely chopped broccoli stalks (about ¾ pound
    stalks)
½ cup finely chopped onion
1 teaspoon lemon juice
½ teaspoon salt
¼ teaspoon freshly ground pepper
½ cup grated Swiss or Gruyère cheese
4 eggs, beaten
1 cup half-and-half
Chopped fresh parsley for garnish

Generously butter and coat 6 custard cups, using 2 tablespoons softened butter and ¼ cup bread crumbs. Set aside.

In a 2-quart microwave casserole, combine remaining 1 tablespoon butter, the chopped broccoli, and onion. Cover with lid or vented plastic wrap and cook on High for 6 to 8 minutes, or until tender, stirring after 4 minutes. Add lemon juice, salt, and pepper; stir. Add cheese, remaining ½ cup bread crumbs, eggs, and half-and-half; stir well.

Pour into prepared custard cups. Place cups into the microwave in a circular pattern, allowing 1-inch space between them. Cook on *Medium* (50% power) for 8 to 12 minutes, or until custards are firm and a knife inserted close to the center comes out clean (the center will be creamy but the surface should appear moist with no excess liquid); rearrange dishes after 4 minutes. Remove from oven and allow to stand for 5 minutes before unmolding.

To unmold, cut between custard edge and cup with a sharp knife. Invert a small serving plate on the top of each timbale and turn over quickly to release.

Serve with chopped parsley garnish.

VARIATION
When in season, substitute tender asparagus stalks for broccoli. Reserve 6 asparagus tips. Place in dish with 1 tablespoon water; cover with vented plastic wrap and cook on High for 1 minute. Use as a garnish for timbales.

TIPS
Custards are cooked on Medium because of the sensitive cheese and egg ingredients.

When arranging custard cups, allow at least 1-inch space between them to get the most even cooking.

The unused broccoli flowerets can be cooked and served with lemon butter at another meal.

SERVING SUGGESTION
Serve with Sauce Mornay (page 45) as a first course, or as a main course for a luncheon.

Champignons en Croûtes

Minced Mushrooms in Grilled Bread Rolls

Servings: 12   Preparation time: 35 minutes

1 cup Duxelles (Minced Mushrooms Sautéed in Butter; page
    116)
12 pieces firm-textured white bread
4 tablespoons butter

Prepare duxelles; if prepared in advance and refrigerated, cook
on Reheat (80% power) until slightly warm, about 2 minutes.
    Remove crusts from bread. Place each piece between sheets
of wax paper and roll out to make a thin rectangle, about 4 by
4½ inches and ¹⁄₁₆ inch thick. Place 1 tablespoon duxelles in the
upper half of the rectangle. Keeping duxelles in the upper half,
spread to within ½ inch of the edge. Starting with the filled side,
roll in jelly-roll fashion, to form a finger-shaped roll. Seal edges
with slight pressure. Follow the same procedure with the other
slices.

    Place butter in a custard cup and cook on High for 1
minute, or until melted. Brush melted butter onto the outside
of mushroom fingers with a pastry brush. (At this point mushroom
fingers can be frozen, but remember to add 10 seconds to cooking
time on heated browning dish for each side.)
    Meanwhile, place microwave browning dish in oven and
preheat according to manufacturer's instructions for grilled sand-
wiches, about 5 minutes on High. Place all mushroom fingers

on the heated dish and cook for 35 seconds. Roll fingers over and cook for 35 seconds more, or until golden brown. (All mushroom fingers may not fit on the smaller browning dish. To do remainder, simply reheat dish for original preheat time and cook as indicated above.)

Serve hot.

TIP
Use homemade, bakery, or high-quality store bread.

Moules Marinière Rafraîchies

Steamed and Chilled Mussels

Servings: 6   Preparation time: 20 minutes plus
                                        1 hour to chill

1 medium-size onion, chopped
1 celery rib, chopped
1 garlic clove, minced
1 tablespoon chopped parsley
½ bay leaf, crushed
Pinch of thyme
½ cup dry white wine
3 pounds mussels, cleaned

Combine all ingredients except mussels in a 3- to 4-quart microwave casserole. Cook on High for 3 minutes. Add mussels and cover with lid or vented plastic wrap. Cook for 5 to 6 minutes, or until mussels are opened, stirring after 3 minutes. Discard any unopened mussels. Chill in poaching liquid for at least 1 hour.

Serve chilled in bowls, with poaching liquid spooned on top.

Serve with a Pouilly-Fumé or Muscadet.

TIP
The cleaning of mussels is a distasteful but necessary task if you want to avoid a gritty dirt that will add nothing to this dish. Place mussels in cold water as soon as you bring them home; if necessary, cover the bowl and keep refrigerated until the next day. To clean, discard any broken or slightly open shells. Remove any hard beard with a knife and scrub and wash shells in several changes of cold water. The water should come out clean before the mussels are ready to use.

SERVING SUGGESTION
Serve mussels on the half shell topped with Mayonnaise Moutarde (page 42), or Mayonnaise aux Fines Herbes (page 42).

Mousse de Poisson

Fish Mousse

A refreshing summer appetizer, made lighter with the yogurt variation.

Servings: 8 for first course
         16 to 24 appetizers
         on crackers or toast

Preparation time: 20 minutes
                  plus 3 hours
                  to chill

1 pound fresh or frozen fish fillets (use any mildly flavored white
    fish such as flounder, turbot, whiting, or bass)
1 tablespoon lemon juice
1 tablespoon (1 packet) unflavored gelatin
3 tablespoons cold water
¼ cup mayonnaise (use commercially made or make your own,
    page 42)
4 tablespoons lemon juice
1 tablespoon chopped parsley

1 tablespoon snipped chives
1 teaspoon chopped fresh dill, or ½ teaspoon dried
½ teaspoon salt
Pinch of cayenne pepper
¼ teaspoon freshly ground pepper
1 cup heavy cream, whipped
½ cucumber, unpeeled, fork scored and thinly sliced, or cherry
    tomatoes for garnish
Dill sprigs for garnish

Place fish in a 1-quart microwave dish (10 × 6 inches) or glass pie plate, arranging thicker sections toward the outside. Sprinkle with lemon juice and cover with a paper towel. Cook on High for 5 minutes, or until fish flakes, rotating a half turn halfway through cooking. Drain fish and finely flake with a fork.

In a large glass bowl, stir gelatin in cold water. Heat in microwave for 30 to 40 seconds, or until gelatin is dissolved; stir well. Add mayonnaise, lemon juice, parsley, chives, dill, and seasonings; stir. Add flaked fish and stir. Fold in whipped cream.

Butter a 3- to 4-cup ring mold and spoon in fish mixture. Cover with wax paper and chill for at least 3 hours, or overnight.

Unmold onto a chilled platter and garnish with cucumber slices or tomatoes, and dill sprigs. Serve with crackers or thin slices of toasted French bread.

Serve with a Chablis or a Mâcon-Blanc.

VARIATION
Substitute 1¼ cups yogurt for whipped cream.

SERVING SUGGESTION
Fill center of mousse with Mayonnaise aux Fines Herbes (page 42).

TIPS
Use fish, like whiting, large or small mouth bass, or blue gill, for this recipe.

A paper towel is used to cover fish in cooking because it absorbs some of the released moisture to keep fish drier.

Plat des Légumes Râpés

Grated Vegetable Salad

This might look like a carefully arranged platter of red, green and orange confetti, but the flavor is unmistakably that of crisp marinated vegetables. When placed in concentric circles on the platter, the vegetables can be portioned out with a pie wedge.

Servings: 4   Preparation time: 30 to 50 minutes
                                         plus 1 hour to chill

DRESSING
3 tablespoons vinegar
1½ teaspoons Dijon mustard
1 garlic clove, minced
¼ teaspoon salt
⅛ teaspoon freshly ground pepper
¾ cup olive or peanut oil
1 tablespoon minced parsley, or basil

VEGETABLES
¼ cup water
2 beets, halved
1 bunch of broccoli stems, cut into 1-inch julienne strips
5 medium-size carrots, washed and coarsely grated
½ head red cabbage, coarsely grated

In a small bowl, combine first 5 dressing ingredients; mix well with a whisk. Add oil to the mixture in a slow, steady stream, stirring constantly until well blended. Add herbs and correct seasonings.

   Place 2 tablespoons water and the beets in a 1-quart microwave casserole, cover with lid or vented plastic wrap, and cook on High for 7 minutes, or until tender-crisp. Drain; cool, then peel, and cut into 1-inch julienne strips.

Place broccoli in a 1-quart microwave casserole with remaining 2 tablespoons water. Cover with lid or vented plastic wrap and cook for 3 minutes, until tender-crisp, stirring once. Prepare carrots and cabbage, but do not cook.

Arrange vegetables on a platter in any attractive design. Pour prepared dressing over all. Cover and allow to marinate in refrigerator for at least 1 hour. Serve chilled.

TIP
A food processor can cut the preparation time to a minimum.

Salade de Pommes de Terre au Vin Blanc

Potato Salad with White Wine

Hot potato salad, Lyonnaise style, is served with sausage and mustard as a first course or hors d'oeuvre.

Quantity: about 4 cups

Preparation time: 20 to 25 minutes plus 10 minutes to cool. Allow 1½ hours extra for chilled salad.

3 tablespoons olive oil
2 tablespoons chicken stock
2 tablespoons dry white wine
1 tablespoon lemon juice
1 tablespoon vinegar
1 tablespoon chopped shallot, or sliced green onion
¼ teaspoon salt
Freshly ground pepper
1½ pounds (about 6) waxy boiling potatoes, peeled and cut into
    ⅛-inch slices
Chopped parsley

In a 2-quart microwave casserole, combine all ingredients except potatoes and parsley. Cook on High for 1 minute. Stir well and add sliced potatoes. Cover dish with lid or vented plastic wrap and cook for 6 minutes; stir. Re-cover and cook for 4 to 6 minutes more, or until potatoes are tender; stir in chopped parsley to taste and correct seasonings. Remove from oven and allow to cool, covered, for 10 minutes.

Serve warm, room temperature, or chilled.

SERVING SUGGESTION
Serve with Chair à Saucisse made into patties or links (page 91).

Légumes à la Grecque

Greek-style Marinated Vegetables

These vegetables, blanched in a tangy marinade, will garner accolades for appearance alone.

Servings: 4   Preparation time: 30 to 40 minutes
                                    plus 1 hour to chill

DRESSING
¼ cup white wine
3 tablespoons olive oil
2 tablespoons lemon juice
1 tablespoon chopped shallot, or sliced green onion
1 tablespoon chopped parsley
1 sprig thyme, or a pinch dried
¼ teaspoon salt
⅛ teaspoon fennel seeds, crushed
Freshly ground pepper

VEGETABLES
2 cups sliced mushrooms
2 cups sliced zucchini
2 cups whole green snap beans
1 red pepper, seeds and stem removed, and cut into 1-inch cubes
1 green pepper, seeds and stem removed, and cut into 1-inch
    cubes
Black olives for garnish

Combine all dressing ingredients in a 4-cup glass measure. Add mushrooms. Cook on High for 1 minute; stir. Cook for 1 minute more. Remove mushrooms with slotted spoon to a large serving platter; reserve liquid.

Add zucchini to liquid; cook for 2 minutes. Stir and cook for 2 minutes more. Remove zucchini to platter and reserve liquid.

Add green beans to liquid. Cover with vented plastic wrap and cook for 2 minutes. Stir, re-cover, and cook for 2 minutes more. Remove beans and arrange with other vegetables on serving platter; reserve liquid.

Add peppers to liquid and cook for 2 minutes. Stir and cook for 2 minutes more. Remove peppers and add to platter. Spoon remaining dressing over platter; cover and chill for 1 hour.

Serve chilled with black olives for garnish.

TIPS
The vegetables are being cooked to tender-crisp in the order of increasing flavor strength, so the flavors don't overpower the dressing.

Covering the green beans is necessary so that they will be fully steamed.

SERVING SUGGESTIONS
Serve as first course before for a light luncheon, followed by Timbales de Broccoli (page 19).

Serve as an hors d'oeuvre or salad course.

3

Les Potages
Soups

As we came to know various people in France, we found that there were many stereotypes circulating about Americans. Along with the plaid sports jacket and craving for hamburgers was the certainty that Americans didn't have soup unless it came out of a can—opened by an electric can opener, no less. Well, anyone who thinks that there is a boiling stockpot on the back burner of every French stove is just as mistaken.

There doesn't seem to be time these days to spend all day sweating over homemade soup, yet nothing is more satisfying than serving up a steaming bowl of your homemade brew. The microwave may seem to be the antithesis of the slow-cooking black iron stove, but the fact that the vegetables are so quickly and lightly cooked enables the soup to taste of the stuff of which it's made. It's just the appliance to please the palate, yet satisfy modern time constraints.

Let us add that there is nothing wrong with a canned soup. Yet if you wanted a refreshing chilled cucumber soup, Crème de Concombre Glacée, or a tart apple soup, Potage Ève, or for all you gardeners a daring yet practical violet leaf soup, Potage aux Feuilles des Violettes, chances are that you won't find it in a can.

Because soup plays many roles in a French meal, we've given you quite a selection. There is Fond de Bœuf, which is a beef stock to be used later in cooking. An added benefit is that the meat, which gives the stock its flavor, can be served as a separate course with a Horseradish Hollandaise. Soupe à l'Oignon Gratinée is a hearty main course for winter that brings to mind a roaring fire and robust red wine.

An introduction to a more formal meal might be Potage de Petits Pois à la Française (a creamy green pea soup), or Soupe de Pommes de Terre au Curry.

29

You can't make a silk purse out of a sow's ear. And a soup is only as good as the stock from which it's made. We recommend making beef and chicken stock ahead, to be frozen or refrigerated until the need arises.

Fond de Bœuf

Beef Stock

Quantity: about 4½ cups

Preparation time: 2 hours plus 45 minutes to chill

2 tablespoons cooking oil
3 pounds soup bones, chopped into 3-inch pieces
1 pound beef shank meat or brisket
2 quarts water, or leftover cooking liquid from vegetables
1 medium-size onion, sliced
1 leek, sliced
1 garlic clove, minced
1 celery rib with leaves, sliced
1 carrot, washed and sliced
2 parsley sprigs
4 whole peppercorns
3 whole cloves
1 tablespoon salt
¼ teaspoon thyme

In a 4- to 6-quart microwave casserole, combine oil, bones, and meat. Cook on High for 3 minutes, turn meat over, and cook for 3 minutes more. Add remaining ingredients, cover with lid or vented plastic wrap, and cook for 20 minutes. Stir, re-cover, and cook for 80 minutes. Remove from oven and allow to stand, uncovered, for 10 minutes to cool more quickly.

When stock is cooled, remove surface fat with a spoon. Place stock, uncovered, in refrigerator. Remove meat and any additional congealed fat that forms on the surface. Strain stock. Cover tightly and refrigerate or freeze for later use, or reheat and serve hot as a broth.

TIPS
The hot or cold meat can be thinly sliced and served with Sauce Hollandaise Raifort (page 44), as a luncheon or first course.

Beef stock can be frozen in ice-cube trays to be reheated later for small quantities of soup.

Soupe de Pommes de Terre au Curry

Curried Potato Soup

Servings: 4 to 6   Preparation time: 30 minutes

2 tablespoons butter
1 medium-size onion, finely chopped
2 medium-size potatoes, peeled and cut into eighths
1 tablespoon curry powder
½ teaspoon salt
1½ cups milk
4 tablespoons chopped fresh parsley for garnish

In a 2-quart microwave casserole, combine butter, onions, and potatoes. Cover with lid or vented plastic wrap and cook for 6 to 8 minutes, or until potatoes are soft, stirring once.

With fork or potato masher, mash potatoes and onions together. Add curry powder and salt; mix well. Pour in milk and stir. Re-cover and cook for 2 to 3 minutes, or until almost boiling (do not allow to boil); stir.

· Serve hot or chilled, with parsley garnish.

TIP
To lower calorie content, eliminate butter and cook onion in 1 tablespoon water. Also substitute skim milk for whole milk.

Crème de Concombre Glacée

Chilled Cream of Cucumber Soup

Summer or winter, this soup refreshes and prepares the palate for the meal ahead.

Servings: 6   Preparation time: 25 minutes plus
                                          2 hours to chill

1 tablespoon butter
¼ cup chopped onion
2 tablespoons flour
2 cucumbers, peeled and thinly sliced
1 tablespoon chopped parsley
1¼ cups chicken stock
½ cup heavy cream, sour cream, or yogurt
½ teaspoon salt
Pinch of cayenne pepper
Freshly ground pepper
Sour cream and snipped chives for garnish

In a 3-quart microwave casserole, combine butter and onion. Cook on High for 2 minutes. Stir in flour and mix until smooth. Add cucumbers, parsley, and stock. Cover with lid or vented plastic wrap and cook for 8 to 10 minutes, or until cucumbers are soft, stirring once.

   Pour mixture into a blender or food processor, or force through a fine sieve, and purée. Return to casserole and stir in remaining ingredients except garnishes. Cover and refrigerate for 2 hours to chill.

   Serve each bowl with a dollop of sour cream and some snipped chives.

TIPS
If you need to substitute 1¼ cups of canned chicken broth for

the homemade stock, follow the manufacturer's directions for diluting. Concentrated stock is quite salty.

To speed chilling, place soup in serving bowls, add 1 ice cube to each and place in freezer for 20 minutes. Remove any unmelted ice.

Potage aux Feuilles de Violettes

Violet Leaf Soup

Servings: 4   Preparation time: 30 minutes

2 tablespoons butter
2 medium-size potatoes, peeled and cut into eighths
1 cup fresh violet leaves, without stems, washed and cut into
    ¼-inch strips
1½ cups milk or cream
½ teaspoon salt
Freshly ground pepper
Violet blossoms for garnish

In a 2-quart microwave casserole, combine butter and potatoes. Cover with lid or vented plastic wrap and cook on High for 6 to 8 minutes, or until soft, stirring once. Mash with fork or potato masher.

Add violet leaves, milk, and salt. Mix well. Re-cover and cook on *Medium* (50% power) for 5 to 8 minutes, or until heated through (do not allow to boil), stirring once.

Serve hot with a grinding of fresh pepper. Garnish with a few violet blossoms.

Fond de Volaille

Chicken Stock

When cutting up whole chickens for cooking, save the backs, necks and wings in the freezer until there are enough to make a batch of stock.

Quantity: about 6 cups   Preparation time: 1½ to
                                                      1¾ hours

3 pounds chicken backs, necks, and wings
2 quarts water
6 white peppercorns
1 onion, sliced
2 celery ribs with leaves, sliced
1 carrot, washed and sliced
3 parsley sprigs
1 bay leaf
1 tablespoon salt
½ teaspoon thyme

Combine all ingredients in a 6-quart microwave casserole. Cover with lid or vented plastic wrap and cook on High for 20 minutes. Stir, re-cover, and cook on *Medium* (50% power) for 45 minutes. Remove and allow to stand for 10 minutes uncovered, to cool more quickly. When stock is cooled, strain and remove surface fat with a spoon. Chill, uncovered, in refrigerator. If desired, congealed fat may be removed.

Cover tightly and refrigerate or freeze for later use, or reheat and serve hot as a broth.

TIP
Chicken stock can be frozen in ice-cube trays to be reheated later for small quantities of soup.

Crème de Tomate

Cream of Tomato Soup

Servings: 6   Preparation time: 30 minutes
                                plus 2 hours to chill

1 tablespoon butter
1 onion, finely chopped
1 small garlic clove, minced
1½ pounds (5 to 6 medium-size) ripe tomatoes, peeled, cored,
    and chopped, or 1 can (about 1 pound 12 ounces) plum
    tomatoes, drained and chopped
½ teaspoon salt
⅛ teaspoon freshly ground pepper
¼ teaspoon thyme
2 tablespoons tomato paste
½ teaspoon sugar
1 cup chicken stock
½ cup cream
Tomato slices and chopped parsley for garnish

In a 3-quart microwave casserole, combine butter, onion, and
garlic. Cook on High for 1 minute. Add tomatoes, salt, pepper,
thyme, tomato paste, and sugar. Cook for 7 minutes more,
stirring once.

Pour mixture into a blender or food processor, or force
through a fine sieve, and purée. Return to casserole and stir in
stock and cream; correct seasonings. Cover and refrigerate for
2 hours to chill.

Serve each bowl garnished with a tomato slice and some
chopped parsley.

TIPS
To speed chilling, cover soup and place in the freezer for 30 to
45 minutes.

For ease in peeling the tomatoes, see Ingredients, page 8.

Potage de Petits Pois à la Française

Green Pea and Lettuce Soup

Petits Pois à la Française is the name for the French dish of sweet garden peas steamed in lettuce leaves. The same delightful flavor can be achieved, easily, with this purée of peas and lettuce soup. A grated carrot garnish adds a colorful touch.

Servings: 4   Preparation time: 35 minutes

1 tablespoon butter
1 medium-size onion, chopped
2 cups fresh peas, or 1 package (about 10 ounces) frozen peas, cooked according to package directions
1½ cups chicken stock
2 tablespoons sherry, optional
4 lettuce leaves, coarsely chopped
2 basil leaves, minced, or ½ teaspoon dried
1 teaspoon sugar
¼ teaspoon thyme
Salt and freshly ground pepper
½ cup heavy cream, optional
1 medium-size carrot, pared and grated, for garnish, or snipped lettuce

In a 2-quart microwave casserole, combine butter and onion. Cook on High for 1 minute. Add peas, chicken stock, sherry, lettuce, basil, sugar, and thyme. Cover with lid or vented plastic wrap and cook for 7 to 8 minutes, or until peas are tender, stirring once.

Pour pea mixture into a blender or food processor, or force through a fine sieve, and purée. Return soup to casserole and season to taste. If desired, stir in cream to make a richer soup. Re-cover and cook for 3 to 4 minutes, or until heated through, stirring once.

Pour soup into serving bowls and garnish with grated carrot or snipped lettuce.

TIP
Substitute 1½ cups canned diluted chicken broth for chicken stock.

Soupe de Courgettes au Curry

Curried Zucchini Soup

Curry powder is a blend of many spices including cumin, coriander, tumeric, and fenugreek. Individually, these spices have been part of French cooking from the time of the colonization of Africa and the Far East, possibly even before. The French chef, Roger Lecuyer, once said, "I love to pull the spice drawer open, freeing the Orient. Not a penny changes hands, yet joy undreamed of, I am in magical lands savouring, though unseeing." (*Real French Cooking* by Anthelme Brillat-Savarin, New York: Doubleday and Company, 1957.)

Servings: 4   Preparation time: 25 minutes

2 cups peeled and sliced zucchini
2½ cups chicken stock
⅓ cup dried whole milk
2 green onions, thinly sliced
1 teaspoon curry powder, or more to taste
1 teaspoon lemon juice
½ teaspoon thyme

Place zucchini in a 2-quart microwave casserole. Cover with lid or vented plastic wrap and cook on High for 4 minutes, stirring once. Pour into a blender or food processor, or pass through a fine seive, and purée. Return to casserole and stir in remaining ingredients. Re-cover and cook for 8 minutes, or until steaming hot, stirring once.
    Serve hot.

TIP
Substitute 2½ cups canned chicken broth for chicken stock.

Soupe à l'Oignon Gratinée

Onion Soup with Melted Cheese

We have cut the time in half that it takes to make this classic soup!

Servings: 6　　　　Preparation time: 1 hour

¼ pound butter
4 large onions, peeled and thinly sliced (about 4 cups)
¼ teaspoon sugar
1 tablespoon flour
4 cups beef stock
¼ cup Madeira, or dry vermouth
Freshly ground pepper
6 slices thin French bread, dry or toasted
1 cup (4 ounces) Gruyère or Swiss cheese, grated

Place butter in a 4-quart microwave casserole. Cook on High for 2 minutes, or until melted. Add onions and sugar; mix to coat. Cover with lid or vented plastic wrap and cook for 12 to 15 minutes, or until onions are tender, stirring every 4 minutes.

Sprinkle flour over onions and stir to blend. Add stock, Madeira, and pepper. Re-cover and cook for 10 to 12 minutes, or until bubbling, stirring halfway through.

Divide soup among 6 bowls. Place a slice of bread on top of each bowl and sprinkle each with cheese. Place bowls in microwave oven in a circular pattern. Cook for 6 to 8 minutes, or until cheese melts, repositioning bowls halfway through if necessary. Serve.

TIPS
Choose the sweeter red or Spanish onions.

Substitute 4 cups canned beef broth. Follow the manufacturer's directions for diluting. Concentrated stock is quite salty.

Potage Fraîcheur

Creamed Spinach, Watercress or Sorrel Soup

This soup can be made from any green leafy vegetable. The word *fraîcheur* connotes anything that is healthy and fresh, and this soup, rich in vitamin C and iron, deserves that title.

Servings: 6   Preparation time: 30 minutes

3 tablespoons butter
¼ cup chopped shallots, or sliced green onions
1 pound fresh spinach, watercress, or sorrel leaves, washed and
    drained
2 tablespoons flour
2 cups chicken stock
1 cup half-and-half
1 tablespoon chopped parsley
½ teaspoon salt
¼ teaspoon marjoram
Freshly ground pepper
Freshly grated nutmeg for garnish

In a 3-quart microwave casserole, combine butter and shallots. Cook on High for 2 minutes. Add spinach and cover with lid or vented plastic wrap. Cook for 4 minutes; stir. Re-cover and continue to cook for 1 to 2 minutes, or until leaves are tender. Place spinach mixture in blender or food processor to chop finely.

Return chopped spinach to casserole and stir in flour until well blended. Add remaining ingredients except nutmeg. Cover with lid or vented plastic wrap and cook for 8 minutes, or until steaming hot, stirring once.

Pour into serving bowls and sprinkle with nutmeg.

Potage Ève

Apple Wine Soup

The childish innocence of Eve as she presented Adam with the first apple was the inspiration for this piquant soup. This startling soup, with a touch of Calvados, will make your guests sit up and take notice.

Servings: 4   Preparation time: 20 to 25 minutes

1 pound tart apples, peeled and cut into thin slices
½ cup water
2 tablespoons grated lemon rind
1 cinnamon stick, or ½ teaspoon ground cinnamon
3 whole cloves
1 tablespoon cornstarch
1 tablespoon cold water
1 cup white wine
¼ cup sugar
1 tablespoon lemon juice
1 tablespoon apple brandy (Calvados or apple jack), optional
Whipped cream, yogurt, or sour cream for garnish
Cinnamon for garnish

In a 2-quart microwave casserole, combine apples, water, lemon rind, cinnamon, and cloves. Cover with lid or vented plastic wrap and cook on High for 6 to 8 minutes, or until apples are tender, stirring once. Remove cloves and cinnamon stick.

In a small dish, dissolve cornstarch in 1 tablespoon cold water; stir into apple mixture. Add wine, sugar, lemon juice, and apple brandy. Re-cover and cook for 5 to 7 minutes, stirring once or twice. Mixture should come to a boil; then stir. Remove from oven and allow to stand 5 minutes out of the oven.

Serve hot or chilled with a dollop of cream, yogurt, or sour cream, and a sprinkling of cinnamon.

4

Les Sauces et les Assaisonnements
Sauces and Dressings

There seems to be an idea in this country that if a recipe is French it must have a sauce. We have had more than one friend secretly admit that he or she avoids certain French restaurants because of feeling suspicious of any food disguised by a sauce.

It is a fact that French *grande cuisine* has fostered an inordinantly large number of sauces, butters, and dressings—well over a thousand. But it's our theory that a sauce should be fairly light, and used sparingly, or not at all if not absolutely necessary. Having said that, when a sauce is properly made and served correctly it will linger on in the memory of a good meal.

There are two sauces that simply can't be excluded: Sauce Hollandaise (egg yolks and lemon) and Sauce Béchamel (basic white sauce). You might find yourself serving them more often than before because they're practically foolproof when done in the microwave. Mayonnaise is incorporated into a number of our recipes and we prefer the recipe here as opposed to mayonnaise from the store. You'll also find that many French sauces are simply variations on a theme. Once you have mastered the basic procedure, flavor changes will involve the addition of only one or two ingredients.

Dessert sauces can add a spark of color as well as flavor. Sauce aux Fraises (strawberry sauce) running down a scoop of vanilla ice cream can make a tantalizing dessert. Sauce à l'Orange is tasty with pork or as a dessert topping for a buttery pound cake.

41

Mayonnaise

Unlike the white custardy mayonnaise sold in your grocery store, this mayonnaise is more like a thick, spoonable vinaigrette; pale yellow in color. It will remind you of the kind that grandmother used to make.

Quantity: about 1 cup   Preparation time: 5 to 10 minutes

1 large egg
¼ teaspoon salt
¼ teaspoon dry mustard
1 tablespoon lemon juice or vinegar
1 cup oil (preferred: ½ cup olive oil and ½ cup vegetable oil)

BLENDER OR PROCESSOR METHOD
In bowl of blender or processor, place egg, salt, and dry mustard; process to mix. Pour in lemon juice and process quickly. As processor is running, pour in oil, in a slow steady stream. Once oil has been added the consistency will be thick and creamy.

BY HAND
In a medium-size bowl, combine ingredients in the same order as above, beating with fork or whisk after each addition. When it comes to adding the oil, add it in a slow, steady stream, beating constantly with a whisk.
     Keep refrigerated.

VARIATIONS
For *Mayonnaise aux Fines Herbes* or Herbed Mayonnaise: Add 1 tablespoon each of the following: finely chopped parsley, basil, chives, or dill; stir. Use as a dip for raw vegetables.
     For *Mayonnaise Moutarde* or Mustard Mayonnaise: Add ¼ cup finely chopped parsley, 1 tablespoon Dijon mustard and 1 teaspoon grated lemon rind; stir.

Aïoli

Garlic Mayonnaise

A type of mayonnaise so popular along the Mediterranean coast it is sometimes referred to as the "butter of Provence." It is often stirred into a fish soup like *bourride,* or used as a dip for vegetables.

Quantity: about 2 cups   Preparation time: 10 minutes

4 to 6 garlic cloves, finely minced
1 tablespoon lemon juice
2 tablespoons dry bread crumbs
4 large egg yolks
1½ cups oil (preferred: 1 cup olive oil and ½ cup vegetable oil)
¼ teaspoon salt
Dash of cayenne pepper, optional

BLENDER OR PROCESSOR METHOD
Make sure that garlic is well minced. In bowl of blender or processor, combine garlic, lemon juice, bread crumbs, and egg yolks; process until thoroughly mixed. As processor is running, add oil in a slow, steady stream. Once oil has been added the *aïoli* will begin to thicken. When all oil has been added, season to taste and process lightly.

BY HAND
In a medium-size bowl, combine bread crumbs and lemon juice; mix into a paste with a wooden spoon. Add garlic and egg yolks to bread-crumb mixture. Add oil in a slow, steady stream, beating constantly with a whisk or spoon until thick. Season to taste.
    Keep refrigerated.

TIPS
The amount of garlic used depends on flavor preference.
    Olive oil is traditionally used for *aïoli,* but we find using some vegetable oil makes the sauce somewhat lighter.

Sauce Hollandaise Raifort

Horseradish Hollandaise Sauce

Quantity: about 1 cup   Preparation time: 5 to 10 minutes

¼ pound butter
1 tablespoon water
1 tablespoon vinegar
3 large egg yolks, beaten
¼ teaspoon salt
1 tablespoon finely grated fresh horseradish, or well-drained
    bottled horseradish
1 teaspoon Dijon mustard

Place butter in a 4-cup glass measure and cook on High for 2 minutes, or until melted. Add water, vinegar, egg yolks, and salt. Beat well with a rotary beater or whisk. Cook on *Medium* (50% power) for 1 minute; beat well. Cook for 1 minute more, or until thickened; beat rapidly.

   Add horseradish and mustard; beat until smooth. Serve warm or cold with boiled beef or chicken.

Sauce Hollandaise

Hollandaise Sauce

Quantity: about 1 cup   Preparation time: 5 to 10 minutes

¼ pound plus 1 tablespoon butter
1 tablespoon water
4 teaspoons lemon juice
3 large egg yolks, beaten
¼ teaspoon salt
White pepper

Place ¼ pound butter in a 4-cup glass measure and cook on High for 2 minutes, or until melted. Add water, 3 teaspoons lemon juice, egg yolks, and salt. Beat with a rotary beater or whisk. Cook on *Medium* (50% power) for 1 minute; beat well. Cook for 1 minute more, or until thickened; beat rapidly.

Add 1 tablespoon butter and beat (this will cool the egg yolks and stop the cooking). Taste and correct flavor with remaining 1 teaspoon lemon juice and white pepper to taste.

VARIATION
For *Sauce Maltaise* or Orange Hollandaise: Add 2 to 3 tablespoons orange juice and 1 teaspoon grated orange rind to 1 cup Sauce Hollandaise.

TIP
If sauce overcooks and starts to curdle, add 1 teaspoon hot water and beat well with rotary beater or whisk.

Sauce Béchamel

White Sauce

Quantity: about 1 cup   Preparation time: 5 to 8 minutes

2 tablespoons butter
2 tablespoons flour
1 cup milk
¼ teaspoon salt
⅛ teaspoon white pepper

Place butter in a 4-cup glass measure; cook on High for 30 seconds, or until melted. Add flour and mix until smooth. Add milk and seasonings; mix with a whisk until smooth. Cook on High for 3 minutes; beat with whisk. Cook for 1 to 1½ minutes more, or until thickened.

VARIATIONS
For *Sauce Mornay* or Cheese Sauce: After removing sauce from oven, add ½ cup coarsely grated Swiss cheese; beat until melted.

For *Sauce Diable* or Mustard Sauce: Place 1 tablespoon butter and 1 tablespoon chopped shallot in a custard cup; cook on High for 1 minute. Add to basic sauce along with 2 teaspoons prepared mustard (Dijon preferred); mix well. (More mustard may be added according to taste.)

Sauce aux Fraises

Strawberry Sauce

Quantity: about 2 cups   Preparation time: 15 to 20
                                                            minutes

1 pint strawberries, hulled, washed, and sliced (about 2 cups)
2 tablespoons sugar
¼ cup red-currant jelly
2 tablespoons Framboise, Kirsch, or other fruit-flavored liqueur
1 teaspoon cornstarch
1 teaspoon water

In a 1-quart microwave casserole, place half of the strawberries and crush with the back of a fork. Add sugar, jelly, and Framboise; stir.

In a custard cup, mix cornstarch with water to form a smooth paste. Add to strawberries. Cook on High for 2 minutes; stir and cook for 2 minutes more until thickened. Stir remaining strawberries into heated sauce. Cool slightly.

Serve warm or chilled over ice cream, custards, or cake.

Crème Fraîche

French Heavy Cream

True French *crème fraîche* is unique to France, but a reasonable facsimile is available now in some large cities. It is cream so thick that a spoon will stand upright in it, with a rich flavor having the slight tartness of sour cream. We call for *crème fraîche* in a couple of recipes.

Here are two recipes from which to choose. The first is simple, but works on the principle for culturing yogurt so it is time-consuming. It also works best in a microwave oven with a food sensor. The second calls for more ingredients, but needs no cooking.

Crème Fraîche I

Quantity: about 1 cup   Preparation time: 8 to 10 hours

1 tablespoon buttermilk
1 cup heavy cream

In a small glass serving bowl, combine both ingredients. Insert microwave food sensor and cook on High until temperature reaches 110°F, about 1 minute. Remove from oven and allow to stand at room temperature for 8 to 10 hours, until cream is thickened. (The warmer and more humid the weather, the less time it will take to thicken. If you have a gas pilot light, let cream stand over this to thicken.)

Crème Fraîche II

Quantity: about 2 cups   Preparation time: 5 minutes

4 ounces cream cheese
½ cup sour cream
1 cup heavy cream

Soften cream cheese for 30 seconds on Medium (50% power).
    In a 4-cup glass measure or bowl, combine softened cream cheese and sour cream. Stir in heavy cream. Refrigerate to store, but to serve bring back to room temperature by heating on Reheat (80% power) for 1 minute.

Sauce à l'Orange

Orange Sauce

Quantity: about 1¼ cups   Preparation time: 5 minutes

¾ cup orange juice
½ cup orange marmalade
2 tablespoons Kirsch, rum, or brandy

Combine all ingredients in a 4-cup glass measure. Cook on High for 3 minutes, or until boiling, stirring once. Serve hot with sausage patties made from Chair à Saucisse (page 91), or hot over pound cake.

Sauce aux Framboises

Raspberry Sauce

This ruby red sauce can be the crowning touch for many desserts.

Quantity: about 2½ cups   Preparation time: 10 to 15
                                                          minutes

3 cups fresh raspberries, or 1 bag (about 12 ounces) frozen
    raspberries, thawed
½ cup sugar
3 tablespoons Kirsch, or Framboise

Place 1 cup berries in a 1-quart microwave casserole. Cover with
lid or vented plastic wrap. Cook on High for 1½ minutes. Pass
cooked berries through a fine sieve to remove the seeds.

Return strained juices and pulp to a 1-quart casserole, adding
sugar and Kirsch. Cook on High for 4 minutes, or until boiling,
stirring once halfway through.

Add remaining 2 cups of whole berries to cooked sauce.
Stir and serve.

5

Les Œufs
Eggs

"Incredible, edible eggs." That's what the advertisements tell us, and when you think about it, they really are. We have summoned their help throughout the book, to leaven our *génoise* cake, thicken mayonnaise and *aïoli,* and bind the sausage filling in Laitues Farcies (stuffed lettuce leaves). But now you've come to the chapter where the egg stands or falls on its own merit, with a little help from some tasty sauces and fillings.

The omelet, although French by conception, has been readily adopted in this country. This versatile egg dish can be presented as a light first course, as in Omelette aux Fines Herbes, or a colorful luncheon dish as in Omelette Basquaise (green-pepper, tomato, and onion filling). It becomes a dessert when folded over apricot preserves and flamed for an Omelette d'Abricot Flambée.

Although eggs are standard fare for breakfast in this country, they are not served for the first meal of the day in France. So we've compromised by giving you some of the familiar poached eggs, without the whirlpool of boiling water, then dressed them up Florentine-style and Diable, to be eaten any time of day. If you've always thought of egg dishes as rather "ho-hum," we challenge you to try Œufs à la Bourguignonne. Present your family or overnight guests with a plate of these shiny poached eggs bathed in a maroon beef and Burgundy sauce. All that will be needed are flowers in a crystal bowl, croissants, and fine china to create an atmosphere equal to that of any fine restaurant.

Omelette Brouillée

Scrambled Egg Omelet

Just as the name implies, the eggs are scrambled in a circular dish and then folded over and served. If a filling is used, it should be small in proportion and shyly tucked away, so as to complement, not overwhelm, the eggs. In cooking omelets on top of the stove it is important to tilt the pan to allow the uncooked egg to run to the edges. This is also important in the microwave, and we follow a similar procedure.

Servings: 1 to 2   Preparation time: 3 to 5 minutes

1 tablespoon butter
3 large eggs, lightly beaten
1 tablespoon cream
⅛ teaspoon salt

Place butter in a 9-inch microwave or glass pie plate; cook on High for 30 to 40 seconds. Meanwhile in a small bowl, combine eggs, cream, and salt. Pour eggs into the buttered plate; cover loosely with wax paper and cook on High for 1 minute. With a fork, break up and move cooked edges along the rim to the center of the dish; the more liquid eggs will flow to the outside. Continue to cook for ½ to 1 minute more, or until center is still slightly moist but set. Using a rubber spatula, lift and fold omelet in half. Slide onto a serving plate.

TIP
These eggs can be cooked on high because the membranes have been broken during beating.

Omelette au Fromage

Cheese Omelet

Servings: 2   Preparation time: 5 to 7 minutes

Omelette Brouillée (page 51)
¼ cup grated Swiss or Gruyère cheese

Prepare omelet, but do not fold.
    Sprinkle cheese on half of the omelet. Using a rubber spatula, lift and fold the half without filling on top of the filled half. Slide onto a serving platter.

Omelette aux Fines Herbes

Herb Omelet

Servings: 1 to 2   Preparation time: 5 to 7 minutes

Omelette Brouillée (page 51)
1 tablespoon mixed chopped fresh parsley, dill, and/or chives

Prepare omelet, but do not fold.
    Sprinkle herbs on half of the omelet. Using a rubber spatula, lift and fold the half without filling on top of the filled half. Slide onto a serving platter.

Omelette aux Fraises ou Framboises

Strawberry or Raspberry Omelet

Servings: 2 to 4 for dessert   Preparation time: 15 minutes

2 tablespoons Sauce aux Fraises or Sauce aux Framboises (page
    46 or 49)
Omelette Brouillée (page 51), omitting salt
2 teaspoons confectioners' sugar, sifted
4 fresh strawberries or raspberries for garnish

Prepare strawberry or raspberry sauce; set aside.
    Prepare omelet, but do not fold. Spoon sauce onto half of
the omelet. Using a rubber spatula, lift and fold the half without
filling on top of the filled half. Slide onto a serving plate. Sprinkle
with confectioners' sugar and garnish with berries.

Omelette d'Abricot Flambée

Flamed Apricot Omelet

Servings: 2 to 4 for dessert   Preparation time: 5 to 6 minutes

Omelette Brouillée (page 51), omitting salt
2 tablespoons apricot preserves
2 tablespoons brandy

Prepare omelet, but do not fold.
    Spread apricot preserves onto half of the omelet. Using a
rubber spatula, lift and fold the half without filling on top of
the filled half. Slide onto a serving platter.
    Place brandy in a 1-cup glass measure; cook on High for
15 seconds. Ignite and pour over omelet.

Œufs Pochés

Poached Eggs

These poached eggs are cooked in individual cups, rather than in one big pot of water on top of the stove. This eliminates the need for the careful stirring of a whirlpool bath on top to keep the eggs in a neat rounded shape.

Servings: 4   Preparation time: 6 minutes plus
                                          2 to 3 minutes
                                          to stand

½ cup water
1 teaspoon vinegar
4 large eggs

Into each of 4 custard cups, measure 2 tablespoons water and ¼ teaspoon vinegar. Cook on High for 1 to 2 minutes, or until water is boiling rapidly.

Break eggs, and gently slide into cups. Cover with vented plastic wrap and place the cups in the microwave in a circular pattern, leaving at least 1 inch of space between the cups. Cook on *Medium* (50% power) for 1½ to 3½ minutes, or until white of egg is opaque but not set; rearrange egg cups once or twice, if necessary. Remove from oven and allow to stand, covered, for 2 to 3 minutes. Jiggle cups, gently, once or twice during standing to help set.

To serve, remove each egg with slotted spoon onto a serving plate, or toast.

VARIATIONS
If you wish to cook 2 eggs at a time, cook on Medium (50% power) for 1 to 1½ minutes, after water has been brought to a boil. For 1 egg, cook on Medium for 45 seconds to 1½ minutes, after water has been brought to a boil.

Œufs Florentine

Poached Eggs with Spinach

Servings: 4   Preparation time: 30 minutes

Epinards au Jus (Spinach Braised in Chicken Stock, page 115)
Sauce Mornay (page 45)
Œufs Pochés (page 54)

Prepare spinach and sauce; cover and set aside.
    Prepare eggs. During standing time, reheat sauce on Medium (50% power) for 2 minutes; stir. Divide spinach mixture evenly among 4 plates. With slotted spoon, place an egg on top of spinach. Spoon ¼ cup sauce over each egg and serve.

Œufs Diable

Eggs with Mustard Sauce

Servings: 4   Preparation time: 15 minutes

Sauce Diable (page 46)
Œufs Pochés (page 54)

Prepare sauce; cover and set aside.
    Prepare eggs. During standing time, reheat sauce on Medium (50% power) for 2 minutes; stir. With slotted spoon, place eggs onto serving plates. Spoon ¼ cup sauce over each egg and serve.

Omelette Basquaise

Omelet with Tomato, Onion, Green-Pepper Filling

Servings: 4   Preparation time: 20 minutes
                                        including all
                                        recipes

1 tablespoon olive oil
¼ cup chopped onion, or shallots
1 green pepper, cut into narrow strips
1 medium-size tomato, peeled and chopped
¼ cup chopped ham
Salt and pepper
Omelette Brouillée (page 51), two recipes to make 4 servings

In a 1-quart microwave casserole, combine oil, onion, and green pepper. Cover loosely with wax paper and cook on High for 2 minutes. Add tomato and ham; stir. Re-cover and cook for 1 to 2 minutes, or until peppers are tender. Season to taste. Set aside.

Prepare one omelet, but do not fold.

Spoon half of the filling onto half of the omelet. Using a rubber spatula, lift and fold the half without filling on top of the filled half. Slide onto a serving plate. Cover and prepare remaining omelet following the same procedure. Cut each omelette in half to serve.

Quiche au Poulet et à l'Avocat

Chicken and Avocado Quiche

Servings: 8 for first course   Preparation time: 1½ hours includ-
          16 for appetizer   ing 1 hour to chill pastry dough

Pâte Brisée (Plain Pastry Dough, page 122)
½ cup cubed cooked chicken
½ cup cubed avocado (about ½ medium-size)
2 teaspoons lemon juice
¾ cup shredded Swiss or Gruyère cheese
3 large eggs, beaten
½ cup half-and-half
½ teaspoon salt
¼ teaspoon freshly ground pepper
⅛ teaspoon freshly grated nutmeg

Prepare pastry dough and roll into a 12-inch circle. Lay dough over bottom of an inverted 9-inch pie plate. Press dough against dish to push out air bubbles, allowing dough to lie flat. Trim dough so that it extends ½ inch over edge of dish. Turn back the extended ½ inch, pressing firmly against the dough shell with the tines of a fork. This will make an edging for the crust. Prick entire surface with a fork every ½ inch or so.

Place pie plate, still inverted with dough side up, in microwave and cook on High for 3 minutes. Rotate a half turn and cook for 2 to 3 minutes more, or until pastry is dry and opaque (pastry will not brown). Remove from oven and allow to cool on dish for 5 minutes. Remove pastry shell from dish and transfer to a serving plate.

Spread chicken and avocado over the bottom of pastry shell. Sprinkle with lemon juice, then with cheese.

In a 4-cup glass measure or bowl, combine remaining ingredients, mixing lightly. Cook on *Medium* (50% power) for 2 minutes; stir. Pour into pie shell and cook for 12 minutes, or until center is set and knife inserted near the center comes out clean, rotating one third turn every 4 minutes.

Remove from oven and allow to stand 5 minutes. Serve hot or cold.

Œufs à la Bourguignonne

Eggs in Burgundy Sauce

Before you flip the page because you can't imagine eating eggs in Burgundy sauce, give it a second thought. We think you'll fall in love with these eggs swathed in a deep chestnut-colored sauce. Guaranteed to wake up your tastebuds, be it breakfast, brunch, or lunch.

Servings: 4   Preparation time: 20 minutes

¾ cup beef stock
¾ cup dry red wine (Burgundy)
1 bay leaf
1 parsley sprig
1 garlic clove, minced
1 tablespoon finely chopped shallot, or sliced green onion
Pinch ground cinnamon
Pinch freshly grated nutmeg
Œufs Pochés (page 54)
2 tablespoons butter
2 tablespoons flour
4 slices firm-textured white bread, toasted, lightly buttered, and
    cut into circles the size of custard cups
Chopped parsley for garnish

Color page one: (Starting from top) Crème de Tomate, Potage de Petits Pois à la Française, Potage Ève.

Color page two: (Clockwise from top) Pâté de Foie de Volaille surrounded by Pâté en Croûte, Moules Marinière Rafraîchies, Mousse de Poisson with Mayonnaise aux Fines Herbes, and Plat des Légumes Râpés

Color page three: Gâteau au Chocolat and Fraises au Clairet

Color page four: Jambon Braisé à la Normande with Pommes Sucrées and Cream Sauce

In a 1-quart casserole, combine stock, wine, bay leaf, parsley, garlic, shallot, cinnamon, and nutmeg. Cook on High for 10 minutes. Strain and set aside.

Prepare eggs; allow to stand, covered.

Meanwhile, place butter in a custard cup and cook on High for 10 seconds to soften slightly. Add flour and stir into a smooth paste. Beat the paste into strained wine broth with a wire whisk. Cook for 2 to 3 minutes until sauce boils and thickens, stirring once.

To serve: Place buttered toast on 4 heated individual plates. Using a slotted spoon, place 1 egg on each piece of toast; spoon ¼ cup sauce over each. Garnish with parsley.

Serve with a Bourgogne.

6

Les Poissons et les Coquillages
Fish and Shellfish

Say Paris, and one's mind may conjure up a collection of *haute couture*. The city of Marseilles, on the other hand, brings to mind a bustling fish market, which in its own way has as much color and life as any Parisian designer collection. One sees men wearing rolled-up black *pantalons* with blood-stained T-shirts, tattoos, and toothless smiles. One hears the clatter of shellfish being dumped onto wet pavement. The pungent scent of seaweed fills the air, and pesky circling gulls await their share of the catch.

Yet in the midst of all this earthiness the French language can still raise the most plebian-sounding fish to the category of high-brow. Some examples are: *lotte* (monkfish), *merlan* (whiting), *raie* (skate), *roussette* (dogfish) and *colin* (hake). Until the last few years we've dubbed these unfortunate creatures trash fish or underutilized species, yet the French have long been enjoying them. Because they are so inexpensive and available now, when we call for a firm-fleshed fish for Lotte au Pernod (monkfish in Pernod sauce), or Bourride (fish soup), any of the above can be used.

Not that we've limited our scope to these, for scallops, shrimps, and crabs are as popular in France as they are here. Recipes like Crabes à la Diable (deviled crabs) or Crevettes à l'Aneth au Vin Blanc (shrimps in dill and white wine) might appeal more to your tastes.

Crabes à la Diable

Deviled Crabs

The crabmeat and mustard sauce cook into a flavorful soft custard.

Servings: 4   Preparation time: 20 to 25 minutes

5 tablespoons butter
½ cup chopped onion
1 cup and 2 tablespoons milk
2 tablespoons flour
¼ teaspoon salt
Dash of freshly ground pepper
2 tablespoons grated Swiss or Gruyère cheese
1½ teaspoons English or Dijon mustard
2 cans (about 6½ ounces each) crabmeat, drained and flaked
4 tablespoons dry bread crumbs
Paprika

In a 4-cup glass measure or microwave casserole, combine 2 tablespoons butter and the onion; cook on High for 1 minute. Add 1 cup milk, the flour, salt, and pepper; mix well. Cook for 1½ to 2 minutes. Add cheese, mustard, and 1 tablespoon butter; stir. Cook for 1 to 1½ minutes, or until thickened.

Remove ¼ cup sauce to a small bowl. Add remaining 2 tablespoons milk to this portion, stir, and reserve.

Add crabmeat to remaining sauce, and stir. Fill 4 ramekins or coquilles with crabmeat mixture. Spoon the reserved sauce and milk over the filled dishes. Place ramekins in the microwave in a circular pattern, allowing 1-inch space between them. Cook on *Reheat* (80% power) for 6 minutes, rearranging once halfway through. Remove from oven and allow to stand.

Meanwhile, place bread crumbs with remaining 2 tablespoons butter on top in a custard cup. Cook on High for 45 seconds, or until butter is melted; stir to blend. Spoon buttered crumbs over each filled dish and sprinkle with paprika. Serve hot.

Serve with a Vouvray or Bourgogne-Meursault.

Coquilles Saint-Jacques Minceur

Scallops in Wine

Scallops are often prepared with heavy cream, cheese, and lots of butter. We decided to let the flavor of the scallops carry this dish and eliminate the cream sauce, hence the title *minceur,* meaning thin or light.

Servings: 4   Preparation time: 15 to 20 minutes

1½ pounds scallops
¼ pound mushrooms, chopped (about 1 cup)
¼ cup chopped parsley
4 teaspoons white wine
4 teaspoons lemon juice
Freshly ground pepper
½ cup dry bread crumbs
4 tablespoons butter

Divide scallops among 4 ramekins or coquilles (shells), topping each with equal portions of mushrooms and parsley. Sprinkle each with wine and lemon juice, then with pepper to taste. Place ramekins in the microwave in a circular pattern, allowing 1-inch space between them. Cover with paper towel and cook on High for 5 minutes. Rearrange dishes and cook for 3 to 4 minutes more, or until scallops are done. Remove from oven and allow to stand.

Meanwhile, in a 1-cup glass measure, place bread crumbs with butter on top. Cook for 1½ minutes, or until butter is melted; stir to blend. Spoon equal portions of buttered crumbs on top of each scallop dish. Serve hot.

Serve with a Châteauneuf-du-Pape Blanc or Bourgogne-Pouilly-Fuissé.

Espadon à la Provençale

Swordfish Provençale

Sunny, boisterous, and bursting with color: these are adjectives that describe Provence, the southeastern-most province of France. The ingredients of that area—tomatoes, garlic, and olive oil—capture that same feeling in this dish.

Servings: 4   Preparation time: 25 to 30 minutes

2 tablespoons olive oil
4 plum tomatoes, peeled, seeded, and chopped (about 1 cup)
1 cup chopped green peppers
2 tablespoons chopped shallots
1 garlic clove, minced
1 tablespoon chopped parsley
2 tablespoons lemon juice
1 tablespoon minced basil, or ½ teaspoon dried
½ teaspoon salt
Freshly ground pepper
2 pounds swordfish steaks

In a 2-quart microwave dish (12 × 8 inches), combine olive oil, tomatoes, green peppers, shallots, garlic, and parsley. Cook on High for 3 minutes; stir in lemon juice, basil, and seasonings. Place swordfish steaks in the dish, with thicker edges toward the outside. Cover loosely with wax paper and cook for 5 minutes. Reposition fish, if necessary, to allow thicker sections to cook more evenly. Re-cover and cook for 3 to 5 minutes more, or until fish flakes. Remove from oven and allow to stand for 2 minutes before serving.

Serve with a Tavel or Côtes de Provence-Rosé.

TIP
For ease in peeling tomatoes, see Ingredients, page 8.

Cabillaud Ménagère

Scrod in Mustard Sauce

Ménagère, as a cooking term loosely translated, means "thrifty housewife." The thought is to spare you the expense, not the flavor.

Servings: 6 to 8   Preparation time: 12 to 15 minutes

3 tablespoons butter
1 tablespoon chopped shallot, or sliced green onion
2 tablespoons dry white wine
2 tablespoons lemon juice
2 pounds fresh scrod or cod
1 tablespoon flour
1 teaspoon dry mustard
¾ cup milk
½ teaspoon salt
¼ teaspoon freshly grated nutmeg
Freshly ground pepper

In a 2-quart microwave dish (12 × 8 inches), combine 2 tablespoons butter and the shallot. Cook on High for 1 minute. Add wine and lemon juice; arrange fish in same casserole, with thicker edges toward the outside. Cover loosely with wax paper. Cook for 8 to 10 minutes, or until fish flakes easily, repositioning fish, if necessary, to allow the thicker sections to cook more evenly. With a slotted spoon, transfer fish to a serving platter and allow to stand, covered. Strain pan juices and set them aside.

Put remaining 1 tablespoon butter into the empty 2-quart dish. Cook for 30 to 45 seconds, or until melted. Add flour and dry mustard; stir until smooth. Add strained pan juices; stir. Add milk and seasonings; stir again. Cook for 1 to 2 minutes, until slightly thickened, stirring halfway through. Pour sauce over fish and serve.

Serve with a Bordeaux-Blanc or Loire-Blanc.

Lotte au Pernod

Monkfish in Pernod Sauce

Lotte, known as monkfish or goosefish in this country, is an ugly, black-skinned fish. The large, grotesque head is never used because fishermen feel that since God has not been kind to this creature, its presence will surely bring bad luck; so the head unceremoniously receives a burial at sea. The pale pink fillets, on the other hand, are worthy of careful preparation in white wine or liqueur. We've prepared them here with anise-flavored Pernod.

Servings: 4   Preparation time: 25 minutes

1 tablespoon butter
2 tablespoons chopped shallots, or sliced green onions
1 garlic clove, minced
1 tomato, peeled, seeded, and chopped (about ½ cup)
2 tablespoons lemon juice
1 tablespoon chopped parsley
½ teaspoon salt
¼ teaspoon freshly ground pepper
2 pounds monkfish or other firm fish, cleaned, boned, skinned, and cut into 2-inch cubes
1 tablespoon Pernod or other anise-flavored liqueur
1 tablespoon capers for garnish
Lemon wedges for garnish

In a 2-quart microwave dish (12 × 8 inches), combine butter, shallots, and garlic. Cook on High for 2 minutes. Add tomato, lemon juice, parsley, salt, and pepper; cook for 2 minutes. Add fish cubes and Pernod; mix to coat fish with sauce. Cover loosely with wax paper. Cook for 4 minutes; stir to reposition fish cubes from the outside to the inside. Re-cover and cook for 4 to 6 minutes more, or until fish flakes.

Serve in individual bowls with capers and a lemon wedge.
Serve with a Bourgogne-Blanc or Rhône-Hermitage Blanc.

SERVING SUGGESTION
Good as a simple dinner with crusty French bread and a green salad.

TIP
For ease in peeling tomatoes, see Ingredients, page 8.

Crevettes à l'Aneth au Vin Blanc

Shrimps in Dill and White Wine

Servings: 4   Preparation time: 10 to 15 minutes

1 tablespoon chopped parsley
4 sprigs fresh dill, without stems
1 bay leaf
1 garlic clove, minced
½ teaspoon salt
¼ teaspoon thyme
Freshly ground pepper
1 cup dry white wine
1 tablespoon lemon juice
1½ pounds medium shrimps, washed but not peeled

Place all ingredients in a 2-quart microwave casserole; stir to coat shrimps. Cover with lid or vented plastic wrap and cook on High for 4 minutes. Stir, moving shrimps from the outside edges to the inside. Re-cover and cook for 2 to 4 minutes more, or until shrimps are pink. (Be careful not to overcook.)

Remove bay leaf and dill. Serve shrimps in soup bowls, with some of the hot broth spooned on top. Peel each shrimp, dipping into broth before eating.

Serve with a Rhône-Hermitage Blanc or Bordeaux-Entre-deux-Mers.

SERVING SUGGESTION
Serve with crusty French bread to dip into sauce. Cooked shrimps may be served with melted butter for dipping.

Bourride

Fish Soup

This soup, like the better-known bouillabaisse, hails from the rocky Mediterranean coast, and is to be eaten as a main course. Unlike bouillabaisse, the broth is thickened with a creamy, yellow, garlic *aïoli*.

Servings: 4   Preparation time: 50 minutes

BROTH
1 medium-size onion, sliced
1 leek, sliced, or if not available 1 additional onion, sliced
1 pound fish trimmings (bones, heads), plus 2 cups of water (In place of making a stock of this, 2 cups bottled clam juice can be used)
1 cup dry white wine
2 tablespoons chopped parsley
1 bay leaf, crushed
3-inch piece of lemon peel
½ teaspoon salt (eliminate if using bottled clam juice)
⅛ teaspoon thyme, crushed
⅛ teaspoon fennel seeds, crushed

2 cups Aïoli (Garlic Mayonnaise, page 43)
2 to 2½ pounds assorted lean, firm-fleshed white fish (choose 3 or 4 varieties from cod, monkfish, haddock, halibut, sea bass, or hake)
8 slices (about ½ inch thick) French bread, toasted
¼ cup chopped fresh parsley

Combine broth ingredients in a 3- to 4-quart microwave casserole. Cover with lid or vented plastic wrap, and cook on High for 6 to 8 minutes, or until boiling; stir. Cook for 10 to 12 minutes on *Medium* (50% power). Strain broth into a large microwave bowl or casserole (there will be about 3 to 4 cups broth), and set aside. (Broth may be covered and refrigerated or frozen at this point, then brought to a boil later, to add fish about 10 minutes before serving.) Meanwhile, prepare *aïoli*; set aside.

Cover broth with lid or vented plastic wrap and bring it to a boil by cooking on High for 2 to 10 minutes, depending on temperature of broth. Slide fish into hot broth and cook, uncovered, for 6 to 10 minutes, until fish flakes. (Be careful not to overcook fish.)

With a slotted spoon, carefully remove fish from broth and place on a large plate. Cover and set aside.

Meanwhile, place 1 cup *aïoli* in a medium-size bowl or 4-cup glass measure. Gradually, while beating with a wire whisk, add 1 cup hot fish broth to *aïoli*. Slowly pour this mixture back into the remaining hot broth; stir. Cook on *Medium* (50% power) for 4 to 6 minutes, or until mixture thickens slightly and lightly coats a wooden spoon; stir occasionally with a whisk. (Small particles of bread crumbs and minced garlic will be visible.)

To serve: Place 1 or 2 slices of toasted French bread in each soup bowl. Place a few pieces of fish on top of bread. Ladle aïoli-broth on top of fish and sprinkle with parsley. Serve remaining 1 cup *aïoli* at the table, to be added and stirred in, about 1 tablespoon to each bowl, or according to taste.

Serve with a Côtes de Provence-Rosé or Blanc, or Côtes du Rhône.

Loup Farci aux Champignons

Whole Sea Bass with Mushroom Stuffing

Servings: 4   Preparation time: 50 minutes

4 tablespoons butter
2 medium-size onions, chopped
1½ cups soft bread crumbs
¼ pound mushrooms, chopped (about 1 cup)
4 tablespoons chopped parsley
¼ teaspoon salt
¼ teaspoon freshly ground pepper
¼ teaspoon fennel seeds, crushed
1 cup dry white wine
1 carrot, scraped and chopped
1 celery rib, chopped

1 bay leaf, crushed
5 to 6 fresh fennel stalks, about 5 to 6 inches in length, optional
3 pounds whole fish, dressed, with head and tail intact
2 tablespoons Pernod, or other anise-flavored liqueur

In a 1-quart microwave casserole, combine butter and onions. Cook on High for 2 minutes, stirring once. Stir in bread crumbs, mushrooms, 2 tablespoons of the parsley, salt, pepper, and fennel seed. Set aside.

Pour wine into a 3-quart microwave dish (13 × 9 inches), or a serving platter large enough to hold whole fish. Add remaining 2 tablespoons parsley, the carrot, celery, and bay leaf. Cover with vented plastic wrap and cook for 5 to 6 minutes, until liquid is boiling and vegetables are slightly tender. Push vegetables toward the middle of the dish, so that they will be covered by the fish. Arrange fennel ribs on top of vegetables, crosswise and parallel to each other, forming a rack for the fish. Place fish on top of fennel, or if not using fennel, on top of vegetables.

Cover loosely with wax paper and cook for 15 to 18 minutes, or until fish flakes easily in the thickest part, rotating halfway through cooking. Remove from oven and allow to stand 5 to 10 minutes. Meanwhile reheat bread stuffing for 1 minute.

Right before serving, pour Pernod into a 1-cup glass measure or small cup that will be easy for pouring. Heat for 15 seconds. Ignite and pour over fish.

Serve with stuffing and a spoonful of poached vegetables and broth. (The fennel ribs are discarded.)

Serve with a Muscadet or Sancerre.

Poisson en Papillote

Fish Cooked in Parchment Paper

Our guests always derive great pleasure from opening their own parchment packages and inhaling the first fragrances of this dish.

Servings: 6   Preparation time: 35 to 40 minutes

Duxelles (Minced Mushrooms Sautéed in Butter, page 116)
1 cup Sauce Béchamel (page 45)
1 tablespoon chopped parsley
6 sole or flounder fillets (about 1½ pounds altogether)

Cut 6 pieces of parchment paper into heart shapes, about 5 × 8 inches. In a medium bowl, combine *duxelles,* sauce, and parsley.

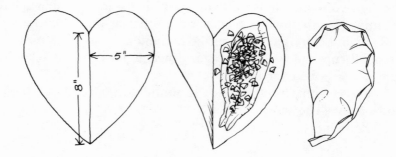

Place each fish fillet on one side of a paper heart. Spoon one-sixth of the *duxelles* and sauce mixture onto each fillet. Fold fish in half if necessary. Fold the parchment in half to cover the fish and crimp the paper edges to close. This should form a tightly sealed packet around the fish and sauce.

Place fish on a microwave dish (9 × 13 inches) or tray, with the thicker edges toward the outside. Cook on High for 7 to 9 minutes.

Serve hot, in paper, for each guest to open individually.
Serve with a Pouilly-Fuissé or Vouvray.

7

Le Poulet
Poultry

"A *poulet* in every pot!" declared Henri IV. This was his goal for every Frenchman in the sixteenth century. During his reign, Henri even appointed a "preparer of *poulets*," as his Minister of State, who was none other than his sister's legendary chef, La Varenne. But the declaration might not have been as straightforward as it sounds.

In those days, *poulet* was a versatile word which could have meant the two-legged barnyard bird, or the more colorful "amorous love letter." What was Henri's real preoccupation with *poulet*? Was he concerned about his countrymen and La Varenne's Affairs of State . . . or did he have his mind on affairs of another sort? For Henri's sister was reported to have said to La Varenne, "you are just as skilled a carrier of my brother's *poulets* as you have been a baster of mine."

Was Henri up to fowl play? Whatever his interest was in *poulet,* ours is strictly in how the *poulet* strikes the palate. We have concerned ourselves with the delicate combination of chicken, green grapes, and white wine to produce the classic Suprêmes de Volaille Véronique. We have smothered chicken in sour cream for Poulet à la Russe, and we have coated it with almonds in Suprêmes de Volaille aux Amandes. There is a reason why we have concentrated mainly on *suprêmes de volaille,* or boneless chicken breasts. They cook quickly and evenly because of their shape and lack of bone. For variety, we have included a Fricassée

Alsacienne, which is chicken parts with onions and mushrooms in a tarragon-flavored white sauce, as well as Coquelets à l'Orange, Cornish game hens with orange sauce.

In all fairness to Henri there is, in fact, a chicken dish which still bears his name: Poule-au-Pot Henri IV, a stuffed chicken, poached in bouillon, in a pot.

Coquelets à l'Orange

Stuffed Cornish Game Hens with Orange Sauce

Servings: 4   Preparation time: 1¾ hours

3 tablespoons butter
¼ cup chopped onion
2¾ cups chicken stock
1 cup raw long-grain rice
2 tablespoons chopped parsley
4 Cornish game hens
Salt
Paprika
4 whole seedless oranges
5 tablespoons water
¼ cup red-wine vinegar
3 tablespoons sugar
1 teaspoon cornstarch
¼ cup Grand Marnier, or other orange-flavored liqueur

In a 2½- to 3-quart microwave casserole, combine 2 tablespoons butter and the onion. Cook on High for 2 minutes to soften onion. Add 2 cups stock and cook for 5 minutes, or until liquid boils. Stir in rice and parsley, cover with lid or vented plastic wrap, and cook on *Medium* (50% power) for 10 minutes. Remove from oven and allow to stand, covered, for 10 minutes. Use later as stuffing for hens.

Meanwhile, prepare hens for stuffing by sprinkling cavities with salt. Fill with rice stuffing and secure cavity shut with toothpicks. Place remaining 1 tablespoon butter in a custard cup and cook for 30 seconds, or until melted. Brush hens with butter and sprinkle with paprika.

Place hens, breast side down, on a roasting rack in a flat 2- to 3-quart microwave dish. Cook on High for 15 minutes, rotating dish one half turn after 7 minutes. Turn hens breast side up and cook for 16 to 19 minutes, or until juices run clear and legs move freely, rotating dish one half turn after 8 minutes.

Transfer hens to a serving platter and cover with foil. Set aside while preparing the orange sauce.

To prepare sauce: Using a vegetable peeler, peel 1 orange, removing only the outer orange zest, not the white. Cut this orange rind into very thin strips. In a 1-cup glass measure, combine orange strips and 4 tablespoons water. Cook on High for 1 minute; drain off water and reserve orange strips.

Peel and section remaining 3 oranges, discarding the peel. Set aside orange sections.

In a 4-cup glass measure, blend vinegar and sugar; cook for 4 to 5 minutes, until syrup is thickened and slightly caramelized. Add remaining ¾ cup chicken stock; stir. In another small bowl, combine cornstarch with remaining 1 tablespoon water; stir until smooth. Stir into syrup and stock mixture, along with orange strips and 2 tablespoons Grand Marnier. Cook for 3 to 4 minutes, or until sauce is slightly thickened.

To serve: Arrange orange segments around the hens on the serving platter. Spoon a little sauce over each hen and pour remainder into a gravy boat. Pour remaining 2 tablespoons Grand Marnier into a small glass cup that will be easy for pouring. Heat for 15 seconds. Ignite and pour over hens. Serve.

Serve with a Beaujolais-Villages or Bordeaux-Rouge.

TIP
The casserole that the rice is cooked in should be twice as deep as the ingredients inside, to prevent boiling over.

Suprêmes de Volaille aux Amandes

Chicken Breasts with Almonds

Servings: 4 to 6   Preparation time: 20 to 25 minutes
                                     plus 5 minutes to stand

1½ pounds boneless chicken breast cutlets, skinned
2 eggs, beaten
4 tablespoons butter, melted
¾ cup very fine dry bread crumbs
½ cup finely ground almonds
4 tablespoons grated Parmesan cheese
1 tablespoon chopped parsley
Lemon slices for garnish

Place chicken pieces between 2 pieces of wax paper and flatten them with a meat pounder to between ¼- and ½-inch thickness.

In a pie or soup plate, combine eggs and butter. In a separate plate, combine bread crumbs, almonds, cheese, and parsley. Dip each piece of chicken into the egg batter and then into the crumb mixture, pressing coating into place with hands.

Arrange chicken pieces with the thicker sections toward the outside of a microwave roasting rack set in a 3-quart dish (13 × 9 inches), or a microwave tray. Cook on High for 4 minutes. Turn over and reposition chicken to allow thicker portions to cook more evenly. Cook for 4 to 7 minutes more, or until chicken is tender and juices run clear. Remove from oven and allow to stand, covered, for 5 minutes. Garnish with lemon slices.

Serve with an Alsatian Gewürztraminer or semi-dry Bordeaux Blanc.

TIP
A microwave roasting rack allows chicken to retain a drier crust by raising it above the dish.

Suprêmes de Volaille Véronique

Chicken Breasts with Green Grapes

Servings: 4 to 6   Preparation time: 25 to 30 minutes

4 tablespoons butter
2 tablespoons flour
½ teaspoon salt
¼ teaspoon freshly ground pepper
½ cup chicken stock
½ cup dry white wine
2 sprigs fresh tarragon, or ½ teaspoon dried
1½ pounds boneless chicken breasts (about 4 large halves), skinned
1 cup seedless green grapes

Place butter in a 2-quart microwave dish (12 × 8 inches). Cook on High for 1 to 2 minutes, or until melted. Stir in flour until smooth. Add salt, pepper, chicken stock, wine, and tarragon; stir well. Arrange chicken with the thicker sections toward the outside. Cover loosely with wax paper and cook for 6 minutes. Turn over and reposition chicken to allow thicker portions to cook more evenly. Re-cover and cook for 6 to 8 minutes more, or until chicken is fork-tender and no longer pink. Transfer chicken to a serving platter; cover.

Place dish with juices back in the oven and cook for 4 minutes, stirring once in the middle of cooking. Add grapes and cook for 2 minutes more. Remove grapes and place around chicken on serving platter. Pour sauce over chicken.

Serve with a Vouvray or Brouilly (Beaujolais-Cru).

Fricassée Alsacienne

Chicken with Onions, Mushrooms, and White Wine

Servings: 4 to 6   Preparation time: 1¼ hours

Salt
Freshly ground pepper
2½- to 3-pound chicken, cut into serving pieces
3 tablespoons butter
½ cup finely chopped onion
2 tablespoons flour
1 garlic clove, minced
2 sprigs fresh tarragon, or ½ teaspoon dried
1 bay leaf, crushed
½ cup dry white wine, or dry vermouth
½ cup chicken stock
Champignons Sautés (Sautéed Mushrooms, page 107)
Oignons au Naturel (Steamed Onions, page 113)
¼ cup chopped fresh parsley

Lightly salt and pepper chicken pieces.
    In a 2½- or 3-quart microwave casserole, combine butter and onion. Cook on High for 2 minutes. Stir in flour until smooth. Add garlic, tarragon, bay leaf, wine, and chicken stock; mix well. Add chicken pieces with the thicker sections toward the outside. Cover with lid or vented plastic wrap and cook on High for 15 minutes. Turn over and, if necessary, reposition chicken pieces to allow thicker sections to cook more evenly. Re-cover and cook on *Medium* (50% power) for 15 to 20 minutes, or until tender. (At this point chicken can be frozen and defrosted later on High for 5 minutes, then on *Medium* [50% power] for 5 minutes; stir.) Reheat on High for 15 to 20 minutes, stirring every 5 minutes or until heated through.
    Remove chicken from oven and allow to stand, covered, while preparing the onions and mushrooms.
    Gently stir the cooked onions and mushrooms into the chicken. Sprinkle with chopped parsley.
    Serve with an Alsatian Sylvaner or Riesling.

Suprêmes de Volaille au Vin Rouge

Chicken Breasts in Red Wine

Servings: 4   Preparation time: 20 to 25 minutes

1½ pounds boneless chicken breasts (about 4 large halves), skinned
¼ teaspoon salt
¼ teaspoon freshly ground pepper
¾ cup dry red wine
1 teaspoon lemon juice
¼ teaspoon thyme
2 shallots, chopped, or green onions, sliced
3 tablespoons butter
2 tablespoons flour
2 tablespoons finely chopped fresh parsley for garnish

Arrange chicken breasts in a 2-quart microwave dish (12 × 8 inches), with thicker sections toward the outside. Sprinkle with salt and pepper. Pour wine and lemon juice over chicken; add thyme and shallots. Cook on High for 5 to 6 minutes. Turn chicken over, and rearrange chicken pieces to allow thicker sections to cook more evenly. Cook for 5 to 6 minutes more, or until chicken is fork tender and no longer pink. Reserving juices, transfer chicken to a serving dish; cover.

   Place butter in a small bowl or 1-cup glass measure and cook on High for 35 to 45 seconds, until melted. Add 6 tablespoons juices and flour to butter; stir until smooth. Return flour mixture to dish and cook for 2 to 3 minutes, until bubbling. Stir and pour sauce over chicken. Sprinkle with parsley and serve.

   Serve with a Morgon (Beaujolais-Cru) or Bourgogne-Pommard.

Poulet à la Russe

Chicken with Sour Cream

We found this recipe a good one to prepare in advance, refrigerate, and reheat. The refrigeration allows the sour cream to permeate the chicken for a delicious flavor.

Servings: 6   Preparation time: 25 to 30 minutes

1½ pounds boneless chicken breast cutlets, skinned
½ teaspoon salt
¼ teaspoon freshly ground pepper
4 tablespoons butter
1 large onion, sliced
½ pound mushrooms, sliced (about 2 cups)
1 cup sour cream
¼ cup dry white wine
¼ cup chopped fresh parsley
Lemon wedges for garnish

Place chicken pieces between 2 sheets of wax paper and flatten them with a meat pounder to between ¼- and ½-inch thickness. Cut each piece into quarters; sprinkle with salt and pepper.

In a 2-quart microwave dish (12 × 8 inches), combine butter and onion. Cook on High for 2 minutes; stir and cook for 1 minute more. Place quartered chicken on top of onion slices with the thicker sections toward the outside. Cover loosely with wax paper and cook for 4 minutes. Stir to allow chicken pieces to cook more evenly; rotate one half turn and cook for 4 minutes more. (Chicken should still be pink inside.)

Add mushrooms, sour cream, and wine; stir to blend. Cook on *Medium* (50% power) for 5 to 7 minutes. Sprinkle with parsley. Serve with buttered noodles sprinkled with poppy seeds; garnish with lemon wedges.

Serve with a Bordeaux-Graves or Mâcon.

TIP
Power is reduced to Medium because of the addition of sour cream.

Suprêmes de Volaille à l'Indienne

Chicken Breasts with Yogurt and Curry

Servings: 4 to 6   Preparation time: 25 to 30 minutes
plus 1 hour for
prefreezing chicken

1½ pounds boneless chicken breasts (about 4 large halves), skinned
2 tablespoons butter
1 medium-size onion, thinly sliced
1 tablespoon flour
2 tablespoons curry powder
½ teaspoon salt
½ cup dry white wine
1 teaspoon lemon juice
½ cup plain yogurt
1 kiwi fruit, sliced as garnish

Slice chicken breasts diagonally into ½-inch slices. (To make slicing easier, place chicken in freezer ½ to 1 hour beforehand.)

In a 2-quart microwave dish (12 × 8 inches) combine butter and onion. Cover loosely with wax paper and cook on High for 2 minutes. Stir in flour, curry powder, salt, wine, and lemon juice; mix well. Place chicken slices on top of this mixture. Re-cover and cook for 5 minutes. Stir chicken into mixture; re-cover and cook for 7 to 9 minutes more, or until chicken is fork tender.

Stir in yogurt, re-cover, and cook for 2 minutes. Garnish with sliced kiwi fruit and serve over rice or buttered noodles.

Serve with a Châteauneuf-du-Pape or Bordeaux-Saint-Émilion.

8

Les Viandes

Meats

Each nationality identifies cuts of meat in a unique manner. To simplify our discussion here, we have categorized meats in two ways—tender and less tender. Tender cuts, like steaks, are quickly cooked by broiling or frying. Tougher cuts of meat that contain more connective tissue should be stewed or braised in the moist-heat method. Fortunately the microwave performs both of these functions extremely well, and in much less time.

But does it brownnnnnn? When meat cooks in the microwave, as in the conventional oven, the outside surface gets hot first and stays hot. Fats rising to the surface are heated and turn brown. What the microwave oven lacks is the dry heat in the oven to form a crisp, dry exterior, but not the ability to brown. And after all, we're roasting meat not coffee beans; the dry heat isn't necessary.

Back to the two types of meat. Microwave cooking is obviously compatible with moist cooking. Braising by the conventional French method begins by cooking the beef, let's say, with stock and vegetables on top of the stove and then transferring the whole lot to the oven to cook for 3 to 4 hours. The idea is to turn a chewy, fibrous piece of meat into one that simply melts in your mouth—a miraculous process that someone can take great pleasure in performing. Probably more miraculous is the fact that someone could find that much time to devote to braising. With the microwave it is easy to cut corners without cutting out flavor.

Microwave cooking helps retain moisture which aids in tenderizing beef. Another help is the use of a Medium power setting to slow down the cooking process. Boeuf à la Mode is a perfect example. A dish that would take 4 hours or more, conventionally, now can be done in under 1 hour. Jambon Braisé à la Normande (braised fresh ham in cream sauce with sugar-glazed apples) and Poitrine de Veau Farcie Marengo (stuffed breast of veal with tomato sauce) are done in a similar fashion. We recommend that the veal be cooked in a water-soaked clay simmerpot to tenderize further.

Steak au Poivre (pepper steak) and Foie de Veau Sauté, Sauce Vermouth (sautéed liver with vermouth sauce) are examples of grilled meats where we've made use of the browning dish to quickly brown and seal in the juices. After cooking, the browned hot juices remain on the dish so that when brandy or Cognac is added the juices can be flamed and served *au jus*. "Flambé," by the way is not merely for show or a pyromaniac's dream come true; A unique and delicious flavor remains after the alcohol burns off which can't be achieved in any other way.

Steak au Poivre

Pepper Steak

Adding Cognac to the sauce and flaming it adds a special and unique flavor.

Servings: 4 to 6   Preparation time: 17 minutes
                                             plus 2 hours for
                                             refrigeration

¼ cup coarsely ground pepper
2- to 3-pound London broil steak, 1½ inches thick
2 tablespoons butter
¼ cup red wine
¼ cup beef stock
2 tablespoons Cognac

About 2 hours before cooking, press pepper into both sides of steak with the heel of your hand. Refrigerate steak.

Place a large microwave browning dish in oven and preheat according to manufacturer's instructions for steak, about 9 minutes on High. Spread butter on heated dish to melt. Add steak to dish and press it down against the dish with a metal spatula. Cook on High for 1 minute. Turn steak over and press down again with a spatula; cook for 1 minute more. (This is done to brown and sear the steak.) Cook for 2 minutes on each side, or until desired doneness is reached.

Transfer steak to a serving platter. To browning dish, add wine and stock, stirring to combine with juices. Cook for 1 minute. Remove browning dish from oven and add Cognac; ignite on the browning dish as Cognac heats.

Serve with a Bordeaux Rouge or Beaujolais.

TIP
The Cognac doesn't have to be preheated before flaming because it becomes hot enough from the browning dish.

Boeuf Bourguignon

Beef Burgundy Stew

Servings: 6   Preparation time: 2 hours
                                    plus 10 minutes to stand

2 thick slices bacon, cut into 1-inch pieces
1 medium-size onion, chopped
1 carrot, peeled and sliced
1 garlic clove, minced
2-pound chuck or rump roast, cut into 2-inch cubes
2 tablespoons flour
½ teaspoon salt
¼ teaspoon thyme
¼ teaspoon freshly ground pepper
½ cup red wine
1 cup beef stock
Oignons au Naturel (Steamed Onions, page 113)
Champignons Sautés (Sautéed Mushrooms, page 107)
Chopped fresh parsley for garnish

Place bacon in a 3- to 4-quart microwave casserole; cook on High for 2 minutes; bacon should still be limp. Add onion, carrot, and garlic; cook for 2 to 3 minutes, or until onion is softened.

In a separate bowl, toss meat cubes with flour; add to casserole. Cover with lid or vented plastic wrap and cook for 5 minutes. Stir in seasonings, wine, and beef stock. Re-cover and cook for 10 minutes; stir. Re-cover and cook on *Medium* (50% power) for 45 to 60 minutes, or until meat is fork-tender, stirring twice throughout cooking. [At this point stew can be frozen, to be defrosted later on High for 5 minutes, then on *Medium* (50% power) for 5 minutes; stir. Reheat on High for 15 to 20 minutes, stirring every 5 minutes, or until heated.]

Remove from oven and allow to stand, covered, for 10 minutes. During standing time, prepare onions and mushrooms. Stir into beef mixture, sprinkle with parsley, and serve.

Serve with a Bourgogne-Rouge-Côte-de-Beaune.

Boeuf à la Mode

Beef Braised in Red Wine with Vegetables

"A French Pot Roast"

Servings: 6 to 8   Preparation time: 2 to 2¼ hours
                                          plus 12 hours to
                                          marinate

Beef and Marinade

3- to 4-pound rump or bottom round roast
2 tablespoons olive oil
2 medium-size carrots, peeled and thinly sliced
1 medium-size onion, finely chopped
1 tablespoon chopped parsley
1 garlic clove, minced
1 cup dry red wine, Burgundy preferred
2 tablespoons vinegar
1 bay leaf, crushed
1 teaspoon salt
¼ teaspoon freshly ground pepper
⅛ teaspoon freshly grated nutmeg
⅛ teaspoon thyme

Rub the meat with olive oil and pierce with fork.

Make a marinade by combining remaining ingredients in a 3-quart microwave dish (13 × 9 inches). Add meat; cover tightly and refrigerate. Marinate for 12 to 14 hours, turning over a few times.

Remove from refrigerator and place dish in oven, covering with lid or vented plastic wrap. Cook on High for 10 minutes; turn roast over. Re-cover and cook for 1¼ to 1½ hours on *Medium* (50% power), or until fork-tender, turning over, and rotating dish one half turn halfway through. Transfer meat to a serving platter and cover with foil. Reserve juices and vegetables; set aside. Prepare vegetables and sauce.

Vegetables

12 ounces baby carrots, or large carrots peeled and cut into 3-inch pieces
1 pound pearl onions, or 3 medium-size onions peeled and quartered
3 tablespoons butter

Combine all ingredients in a 2-quart microwave casserole; cover with lid or vented plastic wrap. Cook on High for 10 to 12 minutes, or until fork tender, stirring once halfway through. Remove from oven and allow to stand, covered, while cooking sauce.

Sauce

1 tablespoon flour
¼ cup beef stock
¼ cup chopped fresh parsley for garnish

While carrots and onions are cooking, take reserved juices and vegetables from meat. With a wooden spoon or mallet force through a strainer into a microwave bowl or casserole. (These vegetables will help to thicken the gravy.) In a small bowl, blend flour with beef stock to make a smooth paste. Add to strained cooking liquid. Cook on High for 4 to 5 minutes, until slightly thickened; stir every minute to make smooth.

To serve, cut beef into thin slices, and arrange carrots and onions around the outside. Spoon some of the gravy over meat and vegetables. Garnish with parsley. Serve remainder of gravy on the side.

Serve with a Juliénas (Beaujolais-Cru) or Côte Rôtie.

TIP
To prepare in advance, cook and slice meat, and arrange on microwave platter. Surround with carrots and onions. Ladle a few spoonfuls of gravy over all. Cover with plastic wrap and refrigerate. To reheat, cook on High for 10 to 12 minutes.

Roulade de Boeuf

Stuffed Beef Roll

Served hot, this pork-filled roll in red-wine sauce makes a tempting main course. Chilled and thinly sliced, without the sauce, the roulade becomes a first course "pâté."

Servings: 4   Preparation time: 40 to 45 minutes
                                      plus 10 minutes
                                      to stand

1 pound round steak, thinly sliced and pounded to ⅛-inch thickness
¼ teaspoon salt
⅛ teaspoon freshly ground pepper
1 pound lean pork, ground
½ cup soft bread crumbs
¼ cup sherry
1 tablespoon chopped parsley
1 garlic clove, minced
½ teaspoon thyme
1 egg, beaten
1 tablespoon butter
1 medium-size onion, chopped
1 tablespoon flour
¼ cup red wine
¼ cup beef stock

Season steak with salt and pepper.
    Place pork in a 2-quart microwave casserole; cook on High for 5 to 8 minutes, or until it loses its pink color. Break up with a spoon and pour off fat. Add bread crumbs, sherry, parsley, garlic, thyme, and egg; mix well.
    Spread mixture on top of steak, spreading to within ½ inch from the edges. Starting with the shorter end, roll in jelly-roll fashion and secure in 3 places with string.

In the same casserole in which the pork was cooked, combine butter and onion; cook for 2 minutes. Add flour and stir until smooth. Add wine and beef stock; mix well. Place rolled steak in casserole, cover with lid or vented plastic wrap, and cook for 5 minutes. Turn meat over and rotate dish one half turn. Recover and cook on *Medium* (50% power) for 10 minutes. Remove from oven and allow to stand, covered, for 10 minutes.

To serve, slice and remove string as you go along. Spoon pan juices over slices and serve hot. Or chill, cut into thin slices and serve as a pâté.

Serve with a Bordeaux-Saint-Émilion or Moulin-à-Vent (Beaujolais-Cru).

SERVING SUGGESTIONS
Serve as a first-course chilled pâté, or begin with Plat des Légumes Râpés (Grated Vegetable Salad, page 25) followed by the roulade.

Bifteck Haché au Poivre

Chopped Steak with Pepper

A simple way to give ground beef a flavor lift.

Servings: 2   Preparation time: 15 to 20 minutes

1 pound ground beef sirloin
½ teaspoon salt
1 tablespoon coarsely ground pepper
1 tablespoon butter
2 tablespoons chopped shallots, or sliced green onions
2 tablespoons brandy
¼ cup beef stock

Form ground meat into 2 oval patties. Sprinkle both sides of each patty with salt. Divide pepper evenly between the 2 patties and press into both sides of each with the heel of your hand.

Place microwave browning dish in oven and preheat according to manufacturer's instructions for ground beef, about 8 minutes on High. Place butter on heated dish to melt. Add patties to dish and press them down against the dish with a metal spatula. Turn patties over and press down again with a spatula. (This is done to brown and sear the patties.) Cook on High for 2 minutes. Turn patties over and cook for 1 minute more, or until desired doneness is reached.

Transfer patties to serving platter. To browning dish, add shallots, stirring to combine with juices. Cook for 1 minute. Remove dish from oven and add brandy; ignite on browning dish as brandy heats. When flame dies down, add beef stock and cook for 1 minute more. Pour sauce over meat and serve.
Serve with a Beaujolais or Côtes du Rhône.

Côtes de Porc aux Tomates

Pork Chops with Tomato Sauce

Servings: 6   Preparation time: 25 minutes plus
                                        5 minutes to stand

2 tablespoons butter
1 medium-size onion, chopped
1 garlic clove, minced
1½ cups peeled, seeded, and chopped tomatoes
2 tablespoons tomato paste
½ cup beef stock
1 tablespoon chopped parsley
1½ teaspoons minced fresh basil, or ¼ teaspoon dried
½ teaspoon salt
¼ teaspoon freshly ground pepper
6 pork chops, each ½ inch thick

In a 2-quart microwave dish (12 × 8 inches), combine butter, onion, and garlic. Cook on High for 3 minutes. Add remaining ingredients except pork chops. Stir to blend. Cover loosely with wax paper and cook for 5 minutes more.

Add pork chops, arranging with thicker sections toward the outside of the dish. Re-cover with wax paper and cook for 6 minutes. If necessary, reposition pork chops to allow thicker sections to cook more evenly. Re-cover and cook for 7 to 10 minutes more, or until chops are cooked through.

Remove from oven and allow to stand for 5 minutes before serving.

Serve with a Cahors or Côtes-du-Rhône Rouge.

TIPS
Wax paper cover on tomato sauce keeps it from spattering the oven.

For ease in peeling tomatoes, see Ingredients, page 8.

Foie de Veau Sauté, Sauce Vermouth

Sautéed Liver with Vermouth Sauce.

Servings: 4   Preparation time: 15 minutes

1 pound calf's liver, sliced approximately ½ inch thick
2 tablespoons butter
½ cup beef stock
2 tablespoons dry vermouth
1 tablespoon finely chopped shallot, or thinly sliced green onion
1 tablespoon chopped fresh parsley
Freshly ground pepper

Remove the surrounding membrane from liver to prevent curling and toughening of outer edges during cooking.

Preheat browning dish according to manufacturer's instructions for meats, about 7 or 8 minutes on High. Spread butter on heated dish to melt. Add liver to dish and press it down against the dish with a metal spatula. Cook on High for 1 minute. Turn liver over and press down again with a spatula; cook for 1 to 1½ minutes on High, until juices from liver run pale rose in color indicating a slightly pink interior.

Transfer liver to serving platter. To browning dish, add stock, vermouth, and shallot, stirring to combine with juices. Cook for 3 minutes, stirring once. Pour over liver and sprinkle with parsley and freshly ground pepper to taste.

Serve with a light Bordeaux or Bourgogne.

Color page one: (Clockwise from lefthand corner) Clafouti Limousin, Tartelettes aux Fruits, Tarte à l'Alsacienne, and (center) Poires Belle Hélène

Color page two: (Clockwise from top) Oeufs Florentine, Oeufs à la Bourguignonne and Oeufs Diable

Color page three: Steak au Poivre and Tomates à la Languedocienne

Color page four: Poisson en Papillote and Asperges au Naturel

Chair à Saucisse

Sausage Mixture

It's hard to buy a good sausage and know exactly what you have purchased. If you have a meat grinder or food processor you can make your own. Sausage, in a French home, may appear as stuffing for a vegetable dish, in a cassoulet, or as sausage links with potato salad.

Quantity: about 3 pounds sausage   Preparation time: 10 to 15 minutes plus 12 hours to chill

2 pounds lean fresh pork (fresh butt)
1 pound fresh pork fat (fatback or fat trimmed from loin roast)
¼ teaspoon dried basil
¼ teaspoon freshly grated nutmeg
¼ teaspoon paprika
¼ teaspoon sage
¼ teaspoon thyme
2 teaspoons salt
½ teaspoon white pepper

Cut meat into 2-inch cubes. Using a food processor or the finest blade of a meat grinder, grind meat with fat. Grind basil, nutmeg, paprika, sage, and thyme together. Blend sausage mixture with seasonings and spice mixture, using a spoon or your hands (dip hands into cold water to prevent sticking). Refrigerate. (The flavor is best when allowed to develop for 12 hours or more.)

TIP
When trimming pork roasts, save fat and freeze for sausage.

SERVING SUGGESTION
Use as a filling for Laitues Farcies, Sauce Champagne (Stuffed Lettuce Leaves with Champagne Sauce, page 96).

Côtes de Porc à la Moutarde et Poires Miellées

Pork Chops with Mustard Sauce and Honey-Glazed Pears

Cook the pears and reheat slightly right before serving the pork.

Servings: 6   Preparation time: 45 minutes

3 tablespoons butter
1 medium-size onion, sliced
1 garlic clove, minced
6 center-cut pork chops
½ teaspoon salt
¼ teaspoon freshly ground pepper
Worcestershire sauce
2 tablespoons flour
½ teaspoon crushed thyme
½ cup chicken stock
1 tablespoon Dijon mustard

In a 2-quart microwave dish (12 × 8 inches), combine butter, onion, and garlic. Cook on High for 3 minutes. Meanwhile, salt and pepper pork chops and rub with Worcestershire sauce.

Stir flour into melted butter. Add thyme, chicken stock, and mustard; stir well. Cook for 2 minutes more.

Arrange pork chops in dish, with thicker sections toward the outside. Cover loosely with wax paper and cook for 6 minutes. Reposition pork chops to allow thicker sections to cook more evenly. Re-cover and cook for 6 to 10 minutes more, or until chops are cooked through. Remove from oven and allow to stand, covered, for 5 minutes.

Serve with Poires Miellées.

Honey-Glazed Pears

2 tablespoons lemon juice
¼ cup honey
3 pears, peeled, cored, and halved

In a 2-quart microwave casserole, combine lemon juice and honey. Cook on High for 1 minute. Stir. Place pears, cut side down, on honey mixture and spoon some of it on top of the pears. Cover with lid or vented plastic wrap and cook for 6 minutes.

Turn pears over; spoon honey on top and re-cover. Cook for 4 to 6 minutes more, or until pears are tender. Remove pears from dish onto serving platter, reserving liquid.

Cook reserved liquid, uncovered, for 4 to 6 minutes more, or until it boils down into a glaze. Spoon over pears.

Serve with a Burgundy-Pouilly-Fuissé or Chablis.

Jambon Braisé à la Normande

Braised Fresh Ham in Cream Sauce with Sugar-Glazed Apples

Normandy is reputedly the source of the best cream in France; after all that's where we get Camembert cheese. The apples are just as well renowned, so we've combined the two to produce this appealing dish.

Servings: 6   Preparation time: 1½ to 1¾
                              hours plus 15
                              minutes to stand

Sugar-Glazed Apple Rings

3 tart apples, peeled and cored, keeping apple intact
3 tablespoons butter
3 tablespoons sugar
1 tablespoon lemon juice

Place butter in a 2-quart microwave dish (12 × 8 inches). Cook on High for 1 minute. Stir in sugar and cook for 1½ minutes more. Meanwhile slice apples into rings.

Place apple rings in butter-sugar mixture and sprinkle with lemon juice. Cover loosely with wax paper and cook for 3 minutes. Turn over apple rings and rotate dish one half turn. Re-cover with wax paper and cook for 2 to 4 minutes more, or until apples are tender.

Remove from oven; turn apples over again and allow to stand in juices until serving time.

Braised Fresh Ham

3- to 4-pound fresh ham, bone removed, rolled and tied
1 teaspoon salt
1 teaspoon freshly ground pepper
¼ teaspoon thyme
2 teaspoons dry mustard
1 medium-size onion, sliced
1 garlic clove, minced
¼ cup dry white wine

With a sharp knife, score outside of pork in a diamond pattern, making about 1-inch diamonds.

Combine salt, pepper, thyme, and mustard; rub into outside of meat.

Place pork, fatty side down, in a 3- to 4-quart microwave casserole or simmerpot. Add remaining ingredients and cover with lid or wax paper. Cook on High for 15 minutes; turn meat over and rotate dish one half turn. Re-cover and cook on *Medium* (50% power) for 40 to 60 minutes, or until meat thermometer registers 170°F, rotating dish one half turn halfway through.

Remove ham to serving platter. Cover with foil and allow to stand for 10 to 15 minutes. (Meat thermometer reading will rise 10° to 15°F during this time.)

Serve with sauce and apple slices.

Serve with a Beaujolais or Bourgueil.

Cream Sauce

Pan juices
1 tablespoon flour
½ cup cream
1 tablespoon apple brandy (Calvados or applejack), cider, or apple juice

Remove as much fat as possible from pan juices. In a small bowl, mix flour with ¼ cup pan juices to make a smooth paste. Return to pan. Add cream and brandy; stir well. Cook on High for 2 to 3 minutes to thicken sauce. Serve with ham.

Laitues Farcies, Sauce Champagne

Stuffed Lettuce Leaves with Champagne Sauce

This dish was born in the aftermath of a bridal shower that left one large bottle of opened Champagne. (It's worth opening a bottle just to try it!) Present the stuffed head of lettuce variation as a first course for six.

Servings: 4 to 6   Preparation time: 40 to 45 minutes

16 lettuce leaves
Chair à Saucisse (page 91) or 1 pound bulk sausage
½ cup soft bread crumbs
1 tablespoon chopped parsley
1 egg, beaten
1 medium-size onion, finely chopped
4 tablespoons butter
1 tablespoon flour
¾ cup Champagne, or combination of white wine and chicken
    stock
1 tablespoon lemon juice
¼ teaspoon thyme
¼ teaspoon salt
¼ teaspoon white pepper
Lemon wedges for garnish

Wash and dry lettuce leaves.
     In a bowl, mix sausage, bread crumbs, parsley, and the egg. Place a rounded tablespoon of stuffing onto each leaf; roll leaf around stuffing and secure with a toothpick.
     In a 2-quart microwave dish (12 × 8 inches), combine chopped onion and butter. Cook on High for 2 minutes. Stir in flour until smooth. Add remaining ingredients except lemon wedges. Cook for 4 minutes. Stir sauce.

Add lettuce rolls, seam side up, to sauce and cover loosely with wax paper. Cook on High for 5 minutes, turn rolls over, and rotate dish one half turn. Re-cover and cook on *Medium* (50% power) for 15 minutes, rotating dish halfway through.

Remove from oven and allow to stand for 5 minutes. Serve with lemon wedges.

Serve with a Champagne or Chablis.

VARIATION
Substitute 1 medium to large-size, firm head of lettuce for 16 separate leaves. Remove tough outer leaves, keeping head intact. Cut opening at the core and remove inner leaves to make room for meat mixture. Stuff hollow head with sausage and cover bottom with lettuce leaf, tucking it into head to secure.

Follow recipe procedure as above and cook head, top side down, on High for the first 5 minutes. Gently turn over and cook on *Medium* for 20 to 25 minutes, or until pork is firm and cooked through. Baste once during cooking.

After standing time, serve whole and cut into wedges at the table. Serves 4 as a main course and 6 as an appetizer.

Poitrine de Veau Farcie Marengo

Stuffed Breast of Veal with Tomato Sauce

This is breast of veal wrapped around a pork stuffing and cooked in a tomato sauce, sweetened with grated carrot. If a clay simmerpot is available, soak it in cold water for 15 minutes.

Servings: 4 to 6　　　　　Preparation time: 1½ hours
　　　　　　　　　　　　　　　　plus 15 minutes
　　　　　　　　　　　　　　　　to soak clay pot

¼ pound Chair à Saucisse (Sausage Mixture, page 91), or bulk
　　sausage
1 cup and 2 tablespoons finely chopped onions
½ cup soft bread crumbs
2 eggs, beaten
¼ pound mushrooms, chopped, or 1 can (about 4 ounces),
　　drained
¼ cup chopped parsley
¼ cup grated Parmesan cheese
6 black olives, chopped
¼ teaspoon rosemary
¼ teaspoon freshly ground pepper
2½- to 3-pound breast of veal, cut with a pocket for stuffing
1 carrot, scraped and grated
1 cup red wine
2 tablespoons tomato paste

Place sausage meat in a 2-quart microwave casserole. Cook on High for 2 minutes. Pour off fat and break sausage into small pieces with a spoon. Add 2 tablespoons chopped onion and cook for 2 minutes, or until onion is softened. Add bread crumbs, eggs, mushrooms, parsley, cheese, olives, rosemary, and pepper; mix well.

　　Fill veal pocket with sausage mixture. Close with wooden skewers or tie with string.

In a 3-quart clay simmerpot, which has been soaked in cold water for 15 minutes, or a large microwave casserole with lid, combine remaining 1 cup chopped onion, the carrot, red wine, and tomato paste; mix well. Place stuffed veal in dish and cover with lid. Cook on High for 15 minutes. Turn meat over, re-cover, and cook for 50 to 60 minutes on *Medium* (50% power), or until meat is tender.

Remove from oven and allow to stand, covered, for 10 minutes.

To serve, slice between bones; serve with a spoonful of the vegetables from the cooking dish; they will be reduced to a purée.

Serve with a light Bourgogne or Rosé d'Anjou.

TIP
A simmerpot will retain more of the juices, and help to tenderize the meat.

Paupiettes de Veau au Jambon et Fromage

Veal Rolls with Ham and Cheese

Servings: 6   Preparation time: 35 minutes plus
                                        5 minutes to stand

6 veal cutlets (about 1 pound), pounded to 1/8-inch thickness
6 thin slices boiled ham
6 thin slices Swiss cheese
6 fresh basil leaves
1 tablespoon chopped parsley
1 tablespoon snipped chives
2 tablespoons flour
1/2 teaspoon salt
1/4 teaspoon freshly ground pepper
2 tablespoons butter
2 tablespoons brandy
1/2 cup beef stock

Layer each cutlet with 1 slice of ham, 1 slice of cheese, 1 basil leaf, and a sprinkling of parsley and chives. Roll in jelly-roll fashion and tie with a string at both ends. Sprinkle with flour, salt, and pepper.

Place microwave browning dish in oven and preheat according to manufacturer's instructions for veal or steak, about 8 minutes on High. Spread butter on heated dish to melt. Add veal rolls and press them down against the dish with a metal spatula. Cook for 1 minute. Turn rolls over and press down again with spatula; cook for 1 minute more.

Transfer veal rolls to another plate. Remove browning dish from oven and add brandy; ignite on the browning dish as brandy heats. When flame dies down, add beef stock; stir. If browning dish is a casserole with lid, place veal rolls back in browning dish and cook for 2 minutes. Cover with lid and cook on *Medium* (50% power) for 5 minutes more.

If browning dish is a flat skillet, then combine sauce and veal rolls in a 2-quart microwave casserole. Cook on High for 2 minutes, then cover and cook on *Medium* for 5 minutes more.

Allow to stand for 5 minutes before serving.
Serve with a Bordeaux-Rouge or Beaujolais.

Veau Poêlé

Roasted Veal Casserole

Veal is often "larded" or threaded with lard on the inside because it is such a lean meat. Instead we've added bacon strips on top to increase the fat. If a clay simmerpot is available, soak it in cold water for 15 minutes.

Servings: 6   Preparation time: 1¾ hours plus 15
                     minutes to soak clay pot

2 strips bacon
3-pound veal roast, boned and tied
2 carrots, peeled and thinly sliced
2 medium-size onions, thinly sliced (about 2 cups)
1 tablespoon chopped parsley
½ teaspoon salt
¼ teaspoon thyme
¼ teaspoon freshly ground pepper
1 cup chicken stock
⅓ cup Madeira, or sweet vermouth
1 tablespoon cornstarch
¼ pound sliced fresh mushrooms (about 1 cup)

Place bacon between paper towels and place on a paper or microwave-proof plate. Cook on High for 1 minute to cook partially. Place veal in a 3-quart clay simmerpot, which has been soaking for 15 minutes, or a large microwave casserole with lid. Cover and cook on High for 15 minutes, rotating one half turn halfway through.

Turn meat over and add carrots, onions, parsley, and seasonings. Place bacon on top of meat. Re-cover and cook on *Medium* (50% power) for 50 to 60 minutes, or until veal reaches 160°F. Turn meat over once halfway through cooking and baste as needed.

Reserve juices in casserole, and transfer meat to a serving platter; cover with foil.

In bowl or 4-cup-measure, combine chicken stock, Madeira, and cornstarch. Add 1 tablespoon of reserved meat juices and stir until smooth. Add cornstarch mixture to reserved juices in the casserole and cook on High for 8 to 12 minutes, until gravy begins to thicken, stirring occasionally. Remove from oven. Add mushrooms and stir. (At this point veal can be sliced, the sauce spooned over, to be refrigerated for up to 2 days. Reheat and serve.)

To serve, cut meat into ½-inch slices and serve over noodles, with the gravy.

Serve with a Bourgogne-Rouge or Côtes-du-Rhône-Rouge.

Daube à l'Estragon et Basilic

Veal Stew with Tarragon and Basil

These tender chunks of veal and medallions of carrots in a white sauce are flavored with basil and tarragon. If a clay simmerpot is available, soak it in cold water for 15 minutes.

Servings: 6   Preparation time: 1¾ to 2 hours plus
                                           15 minutes to soak clay pot

3 tablespoons butter
1 cup chopped onions
1 garlic clove, minced
3 tablespoons flour
2 pounds boneless veal stew meat, shoulder or breast, cut into
1½-inch cubes
2 carrots, pared and thinly sliced
½ cup dry white wine
½ cup chicken stock
2 tablespoons chopped parsley
2 tablespoons lemon juice
½ teaspoon salt
1 teaspoon minced fresh basil, or ½ teaspoon dried
1 teaspoon chopped fresh tarragon, or ½ teaspoon dried
¼ teaspoon freshly ground pepper
2 tablespoons Crème Fraîche (page 47), or sour cream

In a 3-quart clay simmerpot, which has been soaked in cold water for 15 minutes, or a large microwave casserole with a lid, combine butter, onions, and garlic. Cook on High for 4 minutes to soften onions. Stir in flour to form a smooth paste. Add remaining ingredients and stir. Cover with lid and cook on High for 15 minutes; stir. Re-cover and cook on *Medium* (50% power) for 50 to 55 minutes, or until meat is fork tender. Remove from oven and allow to stand for 5 to 10 minutes.

(At this point stew can be frozen. Later defrost it on High for 5 minutes and then on Medium [50% power] for 5 minutes; stir. Reheat on High for 15 to 20 minutes, stirring every 5 minutes, or until heated.)

Serve with a Beaujolais or Bordeaux-Médoc.

Gigot d'Agneau Persillade

Leg of Lamb with Parsley Crumbs

Leg of lamb turns out beautifully in the microwave. Remember, the French claim lamb is best served *saignant* or still pink. The buttery crumb crust and mustard sauce bring out all the richness of the succulent lamb.

Servings: 6   Preparation time: 35 to 40 minutes plus
                                        10 minutes to stand

2 tablespoons olive oil
2 tablespoons Dijon mustard
4-pound leg of lamb
½ cup soft bread crumbs
2 tablespoons chopped parsley
1 small garlic clove, minced
½ teaspoon salt
¼ teaspoon freshly ground pepper

Gravy

½ cup Beef Stock
1 tablespoon flour
1 tablespoon water

In a small bowl, combine olive oil and mustard. Brush on lamb. In another bowl, combine remaining ingredients except those for gravy, and apply to lamb by pressing on with your hand. Shield the thinner end, which has bone exposed, with foil, folding foil smoothly to cover bone and 2 inches of the meat. Place lamb on a roasting rack in a 3-quart microwave dish (13 × 9 inches) and cook on High for 5 minutes. Turn over and cook on *Medium* (50% power) for about 28 minutes (7 minutes per pound), or until meat thermometer registers 120° to 125°F, rotating dish once after 14 minutes.

Transfer lamb to a serving platter; cover and allow to stand for 10 minutes. Reserve pan juices for gravy.

Meanwhile, in a small bowl combine 2 tablespoons of the beef stock with flour; stir to form a paste. Add to pan juices along with 1 tablespoon water and remaining beef stock. Cook on High for 2 to 3 minutes, or until thickened. Serve with lamb.

Serve with a Bordeaux-Médoc or Hermitage.

9

Les Légumes
Vegetables

Anyone familiar with microwave cooking knows that this appliance treats vegetables with great respect. They are never drowned in volumes of water, or bubbled away until void of flavor and texture. Instead they are cooked to perfection, making vegetables tempting enough to stand alone. And that is the way vegetables are often presented in France. There, it would not be unusual to commence a meal with green beans, mushrooms, or leeks.

More often, though, the vegetable is served as an adjunct to the main course. Because the average cooking time for a vegetable will be about 10 minutes, we recommend that you squeeze in this cooking during the standing time of the main dish. This will give you just enough time to set the table.

We're not sure how much consideration the French give to the retention of nutrients when cooking vegetables. But we are pleased to be able to present vegetables that are delicious, and vitamin-rich too. Cooking vegetables in small amounts of liquid preserves the water-soluble vitamins. If there are any cooking liquids to be drained off, we suggest freezing them for later use in a chicken or beef stock. Because more of the natural flavor seems to remain in the vegetable, you'll be able to use little or no salt for each recipe.

It's true that some vegetables are not terribly subtle when being cooked. They seem to give up the ghost with an odoriferous explosion that can be smelled all over the house. Here's where the microwave comes to the rescue again. You can be sure that you won't be smelling onions or leeks, in the bedroom, two hours after dinner. Now you can go for the pungent vegetables that really have character.

Artichauts au Naturel

Steamed Artichokes

Servings: 4   Preparation time: 20 to 25 minutes

4 artichokes
1 lemon, cut into halves
¼ cup water

Cut off stems, and cut off about 1½ inches from the top of each artichoke. Pull off the few tough bottom leaves, and with scissors snip off tips of each of the outer leaves. Rub entire outside with lemon to prevent discoloration.

In a 2-quart microwave casserole, pour in ¼ cup water and arrange artichokes, base side down. Cover with lid or vented plastic wrap and cook on High for 9½ to 14½ minutes, until lower leaves can be pulled out and the base pierces easily; reposition halfway through cooking. Remove from oven and allow to stand, covered, for 3 minutes.

Drain and serve with Sauce Hollandaise (page 44), or with melted butter and lemon wedges.

Carottes Etuvées au Beurre

Carrots Stewed in Butter

Servings: 4   Preparation time: 15 to 20 minutes

1 pound carrots, peeled and cut into ¼-inch slices
1 tablespoon butter
1 teaspoon sugar
2 teaspoons lemon juice
1 tablespoon finely chopped parsley
⅛ teaspoon freshly grated nutmeg

Combine all ingredients in a 1-quart microwave casserole; stir to coat carrots. Cover with lid or vented plastic wrap and cook on High for 6 to 8 minutes, or until carrots are tender, stirring once halfway through cooking. Remove from oven and allow to stand, covered, for 2 minutes. Serve hot.

VARIATION
Substitute 1 tablespoon Grand Marnier, or other orange-flavored liqueur, for butter and sugar.

Champignons Sautés

Sautéed Mushrooms

Servings: 4   Preparation time: 7 minutes

1 pound whole mushrooms
1 tablespoon butter
1 teaspoon lemon juice
Freshly ground pepper

Remove mushroom stems and reserve for a recipe like Duxelles (page 116). Wipe mushroom caps clean with a damp paper towel. Do not soak them.

In a 2-quart microwave dish, combine mushroom caps with remaining ingredients. Cook on High for 2 minutes; do not cover. Stir and cook for 1 to 2 minutes more, or until just tender. Remove from oven and serve hot.

VARIATIONS
For *Champignons aux Fines Herbes:* Add 1 tablespoon finely chopped fresh parsley, or a combination of 1 tablespoon of finely chopped fresh parsley and snipped chives to mushrooms before cooking.

For *Champignons Diable:* Stir in 1 tablespoon each of Dijon mustard and finely chopped fresh parsley before cooking.

TIPS
Mushrooms should be cleaned only with a damp towel, because peeling or soaking mushrooms in water makes them lose much of their flavor.

Cook mushrooms uncovered, so that they won't turn dark and become too moist. Be careful not to overcook, but to cook until just tender.

SERVING SUGGESTION
Good as an accompaniment with chicken or veal.

Asperges au Naturel

Steamed Asparagus

Servings: 4   Preparation time: 15 minutes

1 pound asparagus
¼ cup water
¼ teaspoon salt

Wash asparagus. Hold each stalk and gently bend until tough end snaps off. Using a vegetable peeler, start right below each tip and peel outer skin to the end of stalk.

In a 2-quart microwave dish (12 × 8 inches), combine water and salt. Place asparagus with buds toward the center. Cover with vented plastic wrap and cook on High for 4 minutes. Reposition spears, moving the outer spears to the middle and vice versa, keeping the buds in the center. Re-cover, cook for 3 to 5 minutes until tender crisp. Remove from oven and allow to stand, covered, for 3 minutes.

Drain and serve with the sauces that follow.

VARIATIONS
For *Asperges Maltaise:* Spoon 1 cup Sauce Maltaise (page 45) over cooked asparagus.

For *Asperges Hollandaise:* Spoon 1 cup Sauce Hollandaise (page 44) over cooked asparagus.

For *Asperges à la Flamande:* Melt 3 tablespoons butter in a custard cup on High for 45 seconds. Add 2 tablespoons fine dry bread crumbs, 1 whole hard-cooked egg, sieved, and 1 teaspoon chopped parsley; stir. Spoon over cooked asparagus.

For *Asperges au Beurre et Citron:* Melt ¼ pound butter in a custard cup on High for 2 minutes. Add ¼ cup lemon juice; stir. Pour over cooked asparagus.

Fenouil au Naturel

Steamed Fennel

Improve your vegetable collection with licorice-flavored fennel, served here with lemon butter or grated cheese.

Servings: 4 to 6   Preparation time: 12 to 15 minutes

2 heads of fennel
¼ cup water

Rinse outside of fennel and trim green tops. Cut each stalk lengthwise into quarters.

Arrange fennel in a 2-quart microwave dish (12 × 8 inches) so that the thicker sections are toward the outside. Cover with vented plastic wrap and cook on High for 3½ minutes. Reposition fennel to allow the thicker sections to cook more evenly. Re-cover and cook for 3½ to 4½ minutes more, or until fork tender. Remove from oven and allow to stand, covered, for 2 to 3 minutes. Drain and serve with the toppings and sauces that follow.

VARIATIONS
For *Fenouil au Beurre et Citron:* Melt 3 tablespoons butter in a custard cup on High for 35 seconds. Add 1 teaspoon lemon juice and pour over cooked fennel. Season with freshly ground pepper.

For *Fenouil au Gratin:* Place 2 tablespoons butter on top of warm fennel; smooth over the top to melt. Sprinkle with 3 tablespoons grated Swiss cheese. Cook, uncovered, on High for 30 seconds or until cheese melts.

Haricots Verts au Naturel

Steamed Green Beans

Servings: 4   Preparation time: 12 minutes

½ pound green snap beans
½ cup water or chicken stock

Wash beans and remove stems and tips, but leave whole. Place beans in a 1½-quart microwave casserole, adding water or chicken stock. Cover with lid or vented plastic wrap and cook on High for 6 to 10 minutes, or until tender-crisp. Remove from oven and allow to stand, covered, for 2 minutes.

If green beans have been cooked in water, drain; if beans have been cooked in chicken stock, serve with stock as "au jus."

VARIATIONS
In a 1-cup glass measure, melt 4 tablespoons butter on High for 1 minute, then:

For *Haricots Verts à la Polonaise:* Stir ¼ cup fine dry bread crumbs and 1 tablespoon chopped fresh parsley into butter. Arrange cooked green beans in serving dish and sprinkle buttered crumbs on top.

For *Haricots Verts Amandine:* Stir 2 tablespoons sliced almonds into butter. Arrange cooked green beans in serving dish and spoon almonds on top.

For *Haricots Verts aux Fines Herbes:* Stir 1 tablespoon lemon juice and 1 tablespoon chopped fresh parsley into butter. Pour over green beans.

Haricots Verts à la Crème

Green Beans with Cream Sauce

Servings: 4   Preparation time: 15 minutes

Haricots Verts au Naturel (preceding recipe)
1 tablespoon butter
1 tablespoon chopped shallot, or sliced green onion
2 teaspoons flour
⅛ teaspoon salt
Freshly ground pepper
Cooking liquid from Haricots Verts au Naturel, plus cream or
    milk to make ½ cup
Chopped fresh parsley for garnish

Prepare green beans according to instructions. Drain, reserving liquid, and allow to stand.

Meanwhile, in a 2- or 4-cup glass measure, combine butter and shallot. Cook for 1 minute on High. Stir in flour, salt, and pepper. Add liquid with cream or milk; stir well. Cook on High for 1 to 2 minutes, or until sauce boils and thickens. Pour over green beans; stir gently.

Sprinkle with parsley.

VARIATION
For a richer sauce use ½ cup cream alone for the sauce liquid.

Poireaux au Gratin

Leeks with Cheese

Leeks are sweet onions, sometimes called the "asparagus of the poor," in France, but they aren't treated that way when cooked with beef broth and grated cheese. So rich they could be a light main dish, or a delightful complement to red meats.

Servings: 4   Preparation time: 15 to 20 minutes

8 leeks (about 2 pounds), untrimmed
½ cup beef stock
3 tablespoons butter
¼ cup bread crumbs
¼ cup grated Swiss cheese

Rinse outside of leeks and trim darker green tops, leaving about 1½ inches of green. Remove roots and the thin layer of yellowish, dried skin on the outside. Insert a small sharp knife into the white base and slice toward the green ends. Split again at right angles to make lengthwise quarters. Rinse under cold water to remove sand.

Arrange in a 2-quart dish (12 × 8 inches) so that the thicker sections are toward the outside. Pour beef stock on top and cover with vented plastic wrap. Cook on High for 3½ minutes. Reposition leeks, moving the outside pieces to the middle and vice versa. Re-cover and cook for 3½ minutes more, or until tender. Remove from oven and let stand, covered, for 3 minutes.

Place butter in a small bowl and cook on High for 35 seconds, or until melted. Stir in bread crumbs and sprinkle buttered crumbs over leeks; top with grated cheese. Cook for 30 seconds to 1 minute, or until cheese is melted. Serve hot.

Oignons au Xérès et Miel

Lightly Glazed Onions

Servings: 4   Preparation time: 15 to 20 minutes

1 tablespoon butter
1 teaspoon vinegar
2 teaspoons honey
½ teaspoon salt
Freshly ground pepper
2 tablespoons sherry, or sweet vermouth
1 pound small white onions (about 1 inch in diameter), peeled

Place butter in a 1½-quart casserole and cook on High for 30 seconds, or until melted. Stir in remaining ingredients. Cover with lid or vented plastic wrap and cook for 5 minutes; stir. Re-cover and cook for 5 minutes more. With a slotted spoon, transfer onions to a serving bowl and cover. Set aside.

Return cooking juices to microwave and cook, uncovered, for 1½ to 2 minutes, or until reduced and thickened slightly. Pour cooking juices over onions and serve.

Oignons au Naturel

Steamed Onions

Servings: 4   Preparation time: 15 minutes

1 pound small white onions (about 1 inch in diameter), peeled
2 tablespoons water
½ teaspoon salt

In a 1½-quart casserole, combine all ingredients. Cover with lid or vented plastic wrap and cook on High for 6 to 8 minutes, stirring halfway through. Remove from oven and allow to stand, covered, for 3 to 5 minutes.

Serve hot with the sauce or topping that follows.

VARIATIONS

For *Oignons Persillé:* Melt 2 tablespoons butter in a custard cup on High for 35 seconds or until melted. Pour butter over cooked onions and sprinkle with 2 tablespoons chopped fresh parsley.

For *Oignons à la Crème:* Combine 1 cup hot Sauce Béchamel (page 45) with 1 tablespoon butter and 2 tablespoons chopped fresh parsley in a 2-quart microwave serving casserole; stir to melt butter. With slotted spoon, add cooked onions and gently fold together with a rubber spatula. Cook on High for 2 to 3 minutes, or until heated through.

Endives Braisées

Braised Endives

Servings: 4   Preparation time: 10 minutes plus
                                              15 minutes to crisp

4 medium-size heads of Belgium endive
2 tablespoons butter
1 teaspoon lemon juice
1 tablespoon beef stock
1 tablespoon finely chopped parsley

Place endives in cold water for 15 minutes to crisp. Drain. Trim the base and remove any tough outside leaves; cut lengthwise into halves.

Place butter in an 8-inch-square microwave dish; cook on High for 35 seconds, or until melted. Arrange endives, cut side up, in butter, placing thicker edges toward the outside. Sprinkle with lemon juice, beef stock, and parsley. Cover with vented plastic wrap and cook for 6 minutes, or until endives are tender, rotating dish one half turn halfway through cooking.

Remove from oven and allow to stand for 2 minutes; serve.

Epinards au Jus

Spinach Braised in Chicken Stock

Servings: 4   Preparation time: 15 minutes

1 pound fresh spinach
1 tablespoon butter
1 medium-size onion, chopped (about ½ cup)
1 tablespoon flour
¼ cup chicken stock
¼ teaspoon freshly grated nutmeg
Freshly ground pepper

Wash spinach well, removing tough stems and cutting leaves into ⅛-inch strips.

In a 3-quart microwave casserole, combine butter and onion. Cook on High for 2 minutes, or until onion is slightly softened. Blend in flour. Add chicken stock and nutmeg; stir. Top with cut spinach and cover with lid or vented plastic wrap. Cook on High for 4 minutes; stir well. Re-cover and cook for 2 to 3 minutes more, or until spinach is tender.

Top with a few grindings of pepper and serve hot.

Duxelles

Minced Mushrooms Sautéed in Butter

Quantity: about 1 cup   Preparation time: 10 to 15 minutes

1 tablespoon butter
1 tablespoon chopped shallot, or sliced green onion
1 tablespoon flour
1 tablespoon beef stock, or Madeira
¼ teaspoon salt
½ pound mushrooms, whole or stems, finely minced (about 2
    cups)

In a shallow microwave dish (9-inch-round, or 8-inch-square),
combine butter and shallot. Cook on High for 2 minutes. Stir
in flour to form a paste. Add beef stock or Madeira, and salt;
stir. Add mushrooms; stir to moisten. Cook for 2 minutes; stir.
Cook for 1 to 2 minutes more, or until mushrooms are steaming
and mixture has formed a moist paste.

   Duxelles can be covered tightly and frozen for 2 weeks.

TIP
Mushroom stems can be used for *duxelles*, reserving caps for
another recipe.

Courgettes Provençale

Zucchini with Tomato, Onion, and Garlic

Servings: 4   Preparation time: 15 to 20 minutes

1 tablespoon butter
1 garlic clove, minced
1 shallot, chopped, or green onion, sliced
2 medium-size zucchini, cut into ¼-inch slices
1 tomato, peeled and cut into ¼-inch slices
¼ teaspoon salt
¼ teaspoon freshly ground pepper
½ teaspoon minced fresh basil

In a 1-quart microwave casserole, combine butter and garlic; cover with lid or vented plastic wrap. Cook on High for 1½ minutes, or until garlic is tender. Add remaining ingredients and stir. Re-cover and cook on High for 2 minutes. Stir outer edges to the inside and cook for 1 to 3 minutes more, or until zucchini is tender. Remove from oven and allow to stand 2 minutes before serving.

TIP
For ease in peeling tomato, see Ingredients page 8.

Pommes de Terre Lyonnaise

Lyonnaise Potatoes

Servings: 6　　　　Preparation time: 20 to 25 minutes

4 tablespoons butter
¼ cup beef stock
4 medium-size potatoes, scrubbed but unpeeled, cut into ¼-inch
　　slices
4 medium-size onions, thinly sliced
¼ cup chopped fresh parsley

Place butter in a 1-cup glass measure; cook on High for 1 minute,
or until melted. Add beef stock and stir well.

　　In a 1½-quart microwave casserole, alternate layers of potatoes, onions, and parsley, and repeat to make 6 total layers.
Pour butter and stock on top. Cover with lid or vented plastic
wrap. Cook on High for 10 to 12 minutes, or until potatoes
are tender, rotating dish one half turn halfway through. Allow
to stand covered for 2 minutes.

Tomates à la Languedocienne

Tomatoes Stuffed with Bread Crumbs and Parsley

A colorful complement to Steak au Poivre.

Servings: 4   Preparation time: 10 minutes

4 firm ripe tomatoes (about 3 inches in diameter)
Salt
Freshly ground pepper
1 slice fresh bread with crust, processed into fine crumbs
3 tablespoons olive oil
1 garlic clove, minced
1 scallion, thinly sliced (about 2 tablespoons)
1 tablespoon finely chopped parsley
1 tablespoon minced fresh basil, or 1 teaspoon dried

Remove tomato stems. Cut tomatoes crosswise into halves; do not cut through the stems. Press outside gently to pop out seeds, leaving interior flesh. Place tomato halves, cut side up, in a 9-inch-round microwave dish. Season with salt and pepper.

In another small bowl, combine remaining ingredients and spoon the mixture on top of tomatoes. Cover loosely with wax paper. Cook on High for 2½ to 3½ minutes, until heated through. Remove from oven and allow to stand, covered, for 2 minutes.

Pommes de Terre au Citron

Potatoes with Lemon

The combination of garlic, lemon rind, olive oil, and nutmeg cooked with the potatoes provides a nice flavor surprise.

Servings: 4   Preparation time: 25 minutes

2 tablespoons olive oil
1 small garlic clove, minced
1 tablespoon finely chopped parsley
1 tablespoon snipped chives
1 teaspoon grated lemon rind
½ teaspoon salt
¼ teaspoon freshly ground pepper
¼ teaspoon freshly grated nutmeg
6 potatoes, peeled and cut into ½-inch cubes
Lemon slices for garnish

In a 2-quart microwave casserole, combine oil and garlic. Cook on High for 1 minute. Add remaining ingredients except lemon and stir to coat potatoes. Cover with lid or vented plastic wrap and cook for 12 minutes, or until potatoes are tender, stirring every 3 minutes. Remove from oven and allow to stand, covered, for 2 minutes.

Serve hot with lemon slices.

10

Les Gâteaux et les Pâtisseries
Cakes and Pastries

The making of cakes and pastries seems to be surrounded by more mystery than any other form of French cooking because of the precise techniques involved. In fact at Le Cordon Bleu in Paris, only two courses are traditionally taught: *Grande Cuisine* which encompasses everything from soup to main courses, and the other solely devoted to *Pâtisseries*. One chef teaches nothing but pastries, and he has been specializing in that for years.

We are not pretending to give you a complete pastry course in this chapter. We simply want to present some easy microwave adaptations for pastries you have been enjoying in French bakeries all these years. Those that we find most adaptable to the microwave are the Génoise (a moist, firm-textured cake), tarts made with Pâte Brisée (a butter crust), and cooked pastry creams and chocolate *couverture*.

We think you'll be pleased with the results and the versatility that the microwave offers.

Pâte Brisée

Plain Pastry Dough

This is the basic unsweetened butter crust for quiches and tarts.

Quantity: pastry for 1 pie   Preparation time: 10 minutes plus
        or 6 tartlets   1 hour to chill

6 tablespoons very cold butter
1 cup flour
½ teaspoon salt
3 to 4 tablespoons ice water

Cut each tablespoon of butter into quarters, to make 24 pieces. In a large mixing bowl, on a countertop, or in a food processor bowl, combine flour and salt; mix well. Add butter with fingertips, pastry blender, or 2 knives. If using a food processor, just add butter pieces to bowl and process quickly. If mixing by hand, work quickly, cutting butter into flour until particles are pea-size.

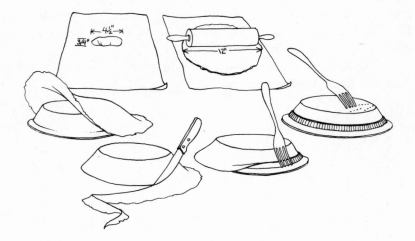

Sprinkle dough with water, 1 tablespoon at a time, and blend quickly, using a tossing motion. Add water only until particles can be gathered into a ball. (Do not overmix or the dough will become tough.)

Flatten the ball into a pancake approximately 4½ inches in diameter (this will make rolling out easier). Cover with plastic wrap and refrigerate for at least 1 hour.

Mixture may be refrigerated at this point for up to 3 days, or frozen. To defrost, place in refrigerator until thawed.

TIPS
It is important to use just the fingertips when mixing the dough with your hands. This is so that no extra heat is added to the dough.

A food processor can be used to blend the dough, but be careful not to overmix.

Tartelettes aux Fruits

Fruit Tartlets

Servings: 6   Preparation time: 1¾ hours including
                     1 hour to chill pastry
                     dough

¾ cup Crème Pâtissière (Pastry Cream, page 136)
Pâte Brisée (Plain Pastry Dough, page 122)
Fresh fruits in season (choose one):
  1 pint strawberries, sliced or whole, *or*
  3 peaches, peeled and sliced, *or*
  ½ pint blueberries and 2 kiwi fruits, peeled and sliced
Nappage (Currant Glaze, page 127)

Prepare pastry dough but shape into a rectangle 6 by 3½ inches; chill for 1 hour.

Roll pastry into a rectangle 16 by 11 inches and cut into six 5-inch circles. Use circles to cover the reverse sides of 6 cups on a microwave muffin pan, pressing dough to edges, or use six 2½-inch diameter ramekins or custard cups, pressing the dough up about 1½ inches on the sides. With tines of fork, press dough edges against sides of cups and prick surfaces with a fork every ½ inch or so. (See illustrations on page 122.)

Place inverted cups, dough side up, in the microwave. Cups should be arranged in a circular pattern with 1-inch space between them. Cook on High for 5 to 6 minutes, or until dry and opaque (pastry will not brown), rotating pan or repositioning cups halfway through cooking.

Remove from oven and allow crusts to cool. Gently remove crusts from cups and trim any uneven edges with scissors.

Fill each cup by spooning in 2 tablespoons cooled Crème Pâtissière. Arrange sliced fruit attractively on top of the pastry cream. Use your imagination in decorating with fruits. Sliced strawberries arranged in a concentric circle are one choice. Whole strawberries, placed with tips up, look very tempting when glazed. Blueberries in the center of kiwi fruit slices are a nice combination.

Spoon or brush warm Nappage over entire surface of tartlet to cover fruit, pastry cream, and upper edge of crust lightly. Refrigerate to chill and set.

VARIATION
A layer of hidden chocolate can be added to the tartlets. Melt 3 ounces semisweet chocolate pieces in a custard cup on High for 1½ to 2 minutes. Spread chocolate on the bottom of cooked and cooled pastry crusts. Allow to harden before adding pastry cream. Then procede with fruit arrangement.

TIPS
When arranging custard cups, the 1-inch space between them is important to get the most even cooking.

When baking pastry shells, check for doneness a minute before the end of cooking time, since crusts will differ in thickness. Look for dry, opaque appearance.

Make individual crusts (freeze crusts if desired) and pastry cream ahead of time, but assemble the tarts no more than a couple of hours before serving, to prevent crusts from becoming soggy.

Tarte à l'Alsacienne

Apple Tart

Servings: 6   Preparation time: 1¾ hours
                                    including 1 hour
                                    to chill dough

Pâte Brisée (Plain Pastry Dough, page 122)
2 tart apples, peeled and sliced to ¼-inch thickness
2 tablespoons plus 1 teaspoon sugar
¼ teaspoon ground cinnamon, plus extra cinnamon
1 egg
¼ cup milk
Nappage (Currant Glaze, page 127)

Prepare pastry dough, sprinkle with flour, and roll into a 13-inch circle. Lay dough over an inverted 9-inch pie plate. Press dough against dish to push out air bubbles, allowing dough to lie flat. Trim dough so that it meets the end of the dish. Turn dough back ½ inch, pressing firmly against the dough with the tines of a fork. This will make an edging for the crust. Prick entire surface with a fork every ½ inch or so. (See illustrations on page 122.)

Place the pie plate, still inverted with dough side up, in microwave and cook on High for 3 minutes. Rotate a half turn and cook for 2 to 3 minutes more, or until dry and opaque (pastry will not brown). Remove from oven and allow to cool on the dish for 5 minutes. Remove tart shell from dish and transfer to a serving plate.

Arrange apples in the shell to form an overlapping, circular pattern in a single layer. Sprinkle with mixture of 1 teaspoon sugar and the cinnamon.

In a small bowl, beat egg, remaining 2 tablespoons of sugar, and milk lightly with a fork. Brush about 1 teaspoon of egg mixture onto top edge of tart; sprinkle edges lightly with cinnamon. Pour remaining egg mixture over apples and cover tart loosely with wax paper. Cook on *Medium* (50% power) for 10 to 12 minutes, rotating a quarter turn every 2 minutes. Custard should be set in the center and apples tender.

Allow tart to cool. Brush with warm currant glaze over entire surface and upper edge of crust.

TIPS
Sprinkling the upper edge of crust with cinnamon gives it a slightly brown appearance.

Cooking the crust on the outside of a pie dish prevents shrinkage and allows for a crust of more even thickness and flakiness.

Crust can be cooked in advance and frozen until apples are to be added.

Nappage

Currant Glaze

Quantity: about ¼ cup   Preparation time: 2 minutes

¼ cup currant jelly

Spoon jelly into a 1-cup glass measure. Cook on High for 2 minutes, or until bubbling and melted. Stir before spooning or brushing onto tarts.

Gâteau au Chocolat

Chocolate-Covered Chocolate Cake

Servings: 8   Preparation time: 1¾ hours
                                   including all cooling
                                   and chilling

Génoise is a fine-textured cake that is firmer and moister than a sponge cake. After baking, the cake is sliced horizontally into thirds, and each layer is dabbed with liqueur and spread with a cream filling before final assembly, when it becomes a *gâteau*.

Traditionally, the cake is made without any added leavening; the heated eggs and sugar which become aerated during beating provide the "lift." Some experts add a little baking powder to insure volume. We have too.

As a cake filling we offer either Crème au Beurre (buttercream, page 130), or Crème Anglaise (custard sauce, page 134). While buttercream may be used for filling and icing, custard sauce is used for filling only. Buttercream is the more traditional choice for filling and icing, but custard filling is thicker and gives a moister cake.

Without reservation this chocolate *gâteau* is an absolute masterpiece. When completely assembled with filling and icing, and glazed with chocolate *couverture,* chocolate triangles, and piped buttercream, it will rival anything to be found in a French bakery. Yet because it is the most involved recipe in the book (notice we said involved not difficult), we stress that you read it through completely before you begin.

Chocolate Cake (*Génoise au Chocolat*)

Servings: 8   Preparation time: 25 minutes plus
                                   15 to 20 minutes
                                   to cool

4 tablespoons butter
5 tablespoons unsweetened cocoa, sifted

3 eggs, beaten
½ cup sugar
½ cup flour
½ teaspoon baking powder
2 tablespoons rum or vanilla extract

Generously coat an 8-inch microwave cake dish with 1 tablespoon softened butter. Dust evenly with 1 tablespoon cocoa.

In a medium-size microwave bowl, combine eggs and sugar; whisk until frothy. Cook on High for 1½ minutes. Remove from oven and beat with an electric mixer or whisk until fluffy, light in color, and thick enough to form a ribbon, about 8 minutes.

Sift together flour, remaining 4 tablespoons cocoa, and baking powder; fold into egg mixture until dry flour or cocoa are no longer visible.

In a custard cup, melt remaining 3 tablespoons butter on High for 45 seconds. Add 1 tablespoon rum or vanilla. Fold the mixture into cake batter, 1 teaspoon at a time.

Pour batter into prepared pan and cook on *Medium* (50% power) for 6 minutes, then on *High* for 1 to 2 minutes, or until cake springs back, rotating ¼ turn every 2 minutes.

Let cake stand on a cooling rack for 15 to 20 minutes before turning out. (The bottom of dish should still feel warm.) Loosen cake with a long-bladed metal spatula, lift up from the bottom, and turn out to cool thoroughly. Meanwhile, prepare Crème au Beurre and allow to chill.

Cut cake horizontally into thirds, using toothpicks all around to mark layers and make cutting easier. Carefully remove top 2 layers. With pastry brush, dab the top side of the bottom 2 layers with remaining 1 tablespoon rum or other liqueur. Reassemble cake and set aside until Crème au Beurre or Crème Anglaise are completely cooled.

In preparation for final assembly, cut a heavy cardboard circle to fit cake, and place under the bottom. (Cake can be wrapped in foil at this point and frozen for up to 1 month.)

TIPS
Génoise is done when cake springs back, although a few moist areas may appear on the top of the cake. These will finish cooking during standing time. The moist areas can be tested for

cake doneness underneath. Touch areas lightly with fingertips. If the cake is done, the moistness that sticks to your fingers will reveal a dry cake below. If the moistness reveals wet batter below, the cake should be cooked for 1 to 2 minutes more.

Air holes may appear on surface, but this is just where some of the steam has escaped during cooking. When turned out, the cake will appear smooth on the surface.

Make sure that the 8-inch dish for the chocolate *génoise* is buttered well before adding cocoa. This is so that the unmolded cake will have a smooth, chocolate crust.

Buttercream (*Crème au Beurre*)

A velvety, rich buttercream that melts in the mouth. The recipe should be doubled if you plan to use it to fill cake layers, ice the outside and decorate.

Quantity: about 1¼ cups

Preparation time: 8 minutes
plus 20 minutes to chill

2 egg yolks
⅔ cup confectioners' sugar
2 tablespoons rum
6 ounces butter, softened

Place all ingredients in a small bowl. Beat with an electric mixer until smooth. Chill until cold but still spreadable.

VARIATIONS
Add ½ ounce chocolate, melted on High for 45 seconds, to the cream after final beating. Beat for another minute, until blended.

Chocolate Glaze (*Couverture au Chocolat*)

A last-minute recipe; prepare the glaze after the cake has been assembled and iced.

Quantity: enough to cover 1 Génoise   Preparation time: 6 minutes

2 ounces semisweet chocolate pieces
1 tablespoon rum
3 tablespoons butter

In a 1-quart bowl, combine chocolate and rum. Cook on High for 1 minute or until melted.

Beat in butter with egg beater or electric mixer. Continue beating until mixture has cooled but still has a pouring consistency, about 5 minutes. Place cake on a cooling rack which sits on top of wax paper, and pour the chocolate glaze over cake, smoothing sides lightly with a knife.

Glazed cake can be refrigerated at this point, in fact it helps to mature flavors.

Chocolate Triangles (*Triangles au Chocolat*)

Quantity: 16 chocolate triangles   Preparation time: 5 minutes
plus 15 minutes to chill

3 ounces semisweet chocolate pieces

Place a sheet of wax paper on a cookie sheet and outline an 8-inch circle with knife. Use a pie or cake pan as a guide.

Arrange chocolate pieces in a circle in a cereal bowl, leaving the center free. Cook on High for 1½ to 2 minutes, rotating one half turn halfway through. Although chocolate pieces still retain their shape they should be just soft enough to spread; test softness with fork. Mash chocolate with the back of a spoon until it forms a smooth paste.

Spread chocolate within circle outline, smoothing with a spatula or knife. Score chocolate circle in half, with knife, and in half again, making sure that wax paper can be seen clearly below cuts. Score each quarter in half and in half again, starting with the center each time, to arrive at 16 wedges. (These scores will be later used to break the chocolate apart.)

Place chocolate in the freezer for 15 minutes to harden. Peel wax paper from chocolate, trimming any jagged edges on the chocolate. Break chocolate at scores and use to decorate *gâteau.*

TIP
The clear definition of knife scores in the chocolate is essential so that they break apart into triangles. If you find that the chocolate breaks unevenly, simply replace wax paper with chocolate into the microwave and heat on High for 2 minutes. Spread to make a smooth circle, score, and refreeze.

It's best to store the chocolate triangles in full circle until you're ready to decorate, to protect the delicate points.

Assemblage of Gâteau au Chocolat

Génoise au Chocolat (Chocolate Cake, page 128)
Crème au Beurre (Buttercream, page 130), plain or chocolate
    variation, or Crème Anglaise (Custard Sauce, page 134) for
    filling
Crème au Beurre, plain or chocolate variation, for icing
Couverture au Chocolat (Chocolate Glaze, page 131)
Triangles au Chocolat (Chocolate Triangles, page 131)
Additional Crème au Beurre for decoration
Toasted chopped nuts, or chocolate jimmies

Final Assembly:

Taking the cake that has been separated into 3 layers, cover the tops of the middle and bottom liqueur-dabbed layers with either:
    a thin layer of Crème au Beurre, or
    about ½ cup of Crème Anglaise for each cake layer.
(If Crème Anglaise is used, there will be some left over which can be spooned on each piece of cake as it is served.)

Reassemble layers onto cardboard circle. With a long-bladed metal spatula cover the top of the cake with a thin layer of Crème au Beurre. Then with a downward diagonal motion, cover the sides of the cake, twirling the cake with the other hand to facilitate icing. Only Crème au Beurre can be used as an outside icing here.

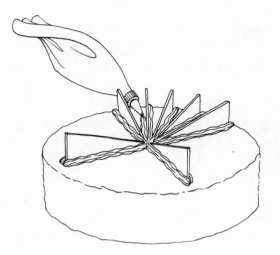

Pour warm chocolate glaze over chocolate cake according to recipe directions.

DECORATION
While glaze is still warm, coat sides of cake with toasted chopped nuts. Hold cake on fingertips of one hand, rotating slowly, while smoothing nuts or chocolate jimmies onto the side of the cake with the palm of the other hand.

Decorate top of cake with Crème au Beurre piped through a pastry bag, and top it with chocolate triangles. (See color photograph also.) Cake can be stored in the refrigerator for 1 week, if it lasts that long!

Serve with Champagne or Saumur.

Crème Anglaise

Custard Sauce (English Cream)

Crème Anglaise is lighter in consistency than Crème Pâtissière, and can be used as a filling or a sauce over poached fruits, or can be chilled and served alone.

Quantity: about 2 cups

Preparation time: 8 minutes plus 30 to 45 minutes to cool

3 tablespoons sugar
1 tablespoon flour
1 cup half-and-half
6 large egg yolks
1 teaspoon vanilla extract, Kirsch, Cointreau, or rum

In a 4-cup glass measure, combine sugar and flour. Beat in half-and-half. Cook on High for 2½ minutes.

In a small bowl, beat egg yolks lightly to syrup consistency. Add egg yolks to half-and-half mixture in a slow steady stream, beating constantly. Cook on High for 30 seconds to 1 minute. Sauce will be somewhat coagulated, but a final beating will smooth it out. Sauce will be slightly thick and creamy.

Remove from oven and beat in vanilla or liqueur. Cool cream, stirring occasionally to prevent a skin from forming. (Mixture may be put in freezer at this point for 30 minutes to speed cooling.)

VARIATIONS
Add a 1-inch piece of vanilla bean to milk during cooking; remove bean before adding egg yolks and eliminate vanilla extract in last step.

For a richer cream, add 1 tablespoon softened butter, after cooling; beat until smooth.

TIPS
If more cooking time is necessary, add in 15-second intervals.

Another way to prevent a skin from forming is to rub the top of the cream, as it begins to cool, with a little piece of butter. The butter will melt from the heat of the warm cream and coat the top.

Covered tightly, the sauce can be stored in the refrigerator for 2 to 3 days.

Use leftover egg whites for Mousse au Citron (Lemon Mousse, page 144).

SERVING SUGGESTIONS
Use Crème Anglaise as a cake filling, or serve in individual wine or sherbet glasses with Sauce aux Framboises (Raspberry Sauce, page 49) spooned on top.

Crème Pâtissière

Pastry Cream

This luscious, pale yellow cream is thickened by egg yolks and flour. Here's a quick and practically foolproof method for making it.

Quantity: about 2 cups   Preparation time: 10 minutes
                                                  plus 30 to 45
                                                  minutes to cool

1½ cups milk
½ cup sugar
¼ cup flour
4 large egg yolks, beaten
1 teaspoon vanilla extract, Kirsch, Cointreau, or rum

Pour milk into a 4-cup glass measure, and cook on High for 3 minutes (milk will be steaming but not yet boiling).

In a separate microwave bowl, combine sugar and flour. Beat in egg yolks. Gradually add warm milk to egg mixture, beating constantly. Cook on High for 1 minute; beat. Cook for 1 to 3 minutes more, or until cream thickens and reaches the boiling point, but do not allow it to boil.

Remove from oven and beat in vanilla or liqueur. Cool cream, stirring occasionally to prevent a skin from forming. (Mixture may be put in freezer at this point for 30 minutes to speed cooling.)

TIPS
Another way to prevent a skin from forming is to rub the top of the cream, as it begins to cool, with a little piece of butter. The butter will melt from the heat of the warm cream and coat the top.

Covered tightly, the cream can be stored in the refrigerator for 2 to 3 days.

Use leftover egg whites for Mousse au Citron (Lemon Mousse, page 144.)

11

Les Desserts
Desserts

You may be wondering why we have separated the desserts from the cakes and pastries. The latter are based on certain doughs and creams that can be used in a number of different ways. Desserts seem to encompass everything else.

So this is our "everything else" chapter where caution can be thrown to the wind and your wildest dessert fantasies realized. For chocolate lovers, there's the airy Mousse au Chocolat and Poires Belle Hélène, poached pears glistening in chocolate sauce. For a hint of intoxication, try Pots de Crème au Rhum, creamy rum custards. For the adventurous there is a rich Sabayon, an egg cream laced with Marsala. And for the faint at heart, there is a lighter-calorie Clafouti, or custard tart made with cherries or apples.

If you enjoy the quest for the perfect dessert, you'll have fun foraging through this chapter. The more serious quester may have to try each recipe two or three times, all in the line of duty, of course.

Poires Belle Hélène

Pears with Chocolate Sauce

We've taken these classic pears one step further by floating them on a light Crème Anglaise. Impressive when served in Champagne glasses.

Servings: 6   Preparation time: 45 minutes
                                      including all
                                      recipes

Crème Anglaise (Custard Sauce, page 134)
6 firm, ripe pears (brown Bosc are preferred for their shape)
1 lemon, cut into quarters
¼ cup sugar
2 tablespoons dry white wine
2 tablespoons Grand Marnier, or other orange-flavored liqueur
Liquid from poached pears, about ⅓ cup
6 ounces semisweet chocolate pieces
2 tablespoons butter, cut into 4 pieces

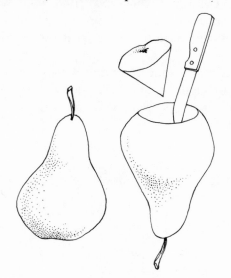

Prepare Crème Anglaise and chill.

Keeping stems intact, core pears so that they retain their shape by cutting into the base in a cone shape with a grapefruit or other small knife. As each pear is peeled, rub with cut lemon to prevent discoloration. Set aside.

In a 1½-quart microwave casserole, combine sugar, wine, and Grand Marnier; mix well. Place pears on sides, positioning the thicker ends toward the outside; add lemon quarters. Cover casserole with lid or vented plastic wrap. Cook on High for 6 minutes. Baste pears and turn them over. Re-cover and cook for 6 to 8 minutes more, or until tender. Drain liquid into a 4-cup glass measure. Allow pears to cool.

The cooking liquid from the pears should measure ⅓ cup. If less than ⅓ cup, add Grand Marnier to correct the amount. (The amount of liquid remaining will depend on the pears and their water content.) Add chocolate pieces to the liquid. Cover with vented plastic wrap and cook on High for 1 minute. Stir and re-cover. Cook for 1 minute more, or until chocolate is melted.

Add butter and beat with a spoon or whisk until mixture has cooled to a spreading consistency, about 5 minutes.

TO ASSEMBLE
When pears have cooled, hold one so that the base with the open core area faces upward. Fill core with approximately 2 tablespoons custard sauce and place pears, base down, in a large dessert dish with a lip, or place each pear in an individual serving bowl. Continue to fill remaining 5 pears in the same manner, and place in the dessert dish.

Surround pears with remaining custard sauce.

Spoon warm chocolate sauce over pears to coat evenly. The excess sauce will run over the custard.

SERVING SUGGESTIONS
The finished pears look particularly nice in a large, cut-glass bowl or individual Champagne or sherbet glasses.

Add a touch of red with Sauce aux Framboises (Raspberry Sauce, page 49).

Sabayon

Egg Cream

Sabayon is a rich egg cream that can serve as an after-dinner "cordial." Good as a last-minute dessert when unexpected company comes.

Servings: 4 to 6   Preparation time: 8 minutes

6 large egg yolks
¼ cup sugar
Pinch of salt
2 to 4 tablespoons Marsala, sweet sherry, or other sweet liqueur

Place egg yolks in a 4-cup glass measure or bowl; beat lightly. Add sugar, beating with a whisk to blend. Cook on Medium (50% power) for 1½ minutes. Whip with a whisk to incorporate air. Cook for 1½ minutes more, whipping every 30 seconds as eggs begin to thicken. When thick and nearly double in volume, add salt and liqueur; beat for 2 minutes until mixture is fluffy.
    Spoon into individual stemmed glasses and serve warm.

VARIATIONS
Reserve the egg whites to make a lighter version of this sabayon. In a bowl, beat 6 egg whites with ¼ teaspoon salt and ¼ teaspoon cream of tartar until whites form stiff peaks. With a wooden spoon, fold whites into warm egg mixture. Spoon into serving glasses.
    If desired, top cream with sliced strawberries or other fruit.

TIP
This recipe needs to be watched closely while it cooks. Make sure to use a Medium power setting, for more cooking control,

and stir often after the first 1½ minutes to prevent coagulation. If more cooking time is necessary, add in 15-second intervals. If mixture does appear coagulated, beat rapidly and add sherry.

SERVING SUGGESTION
Serve each stemmed glass on a doily-lined plate with rolled light butter cookies, called "cigarettes," or a piece of chocolate candy.

Fraises au Clairet

Strawberries in Claret

Servings: 4   Preparation time: 5 to 10 minutes

¼ cup sugar
1 cup claret or Port
2 tablespoons Triple Sec
1 pint strawberries, washed and hulled, or 1 bag (about 10 ounces) frozen unsweetened strawberries, thawed

In a 1-quart microwave casserole, combine sugar, claret, and Triple Sec. Cook on High for 3 minutes, or until sugar is dissolved. Add strawberries and chill. Serve in stemmed wine glasses.

Petits Pots de Crème au Rhum

Individual Rum Custards

Servings: 4　　　　Preparation time: 15 minutes plus
　　　　　　　　　　　　　　　　　　20 minutes to chill

1¼ cups milk
2 tablespoons rum
1 teaspoon vanilla extract
4 large eggs
¼ cup sugar
Fraises Glacées (Glazed Strawberries, page 145)
Mint leaves for garnish, optional

In a 4-cup glass measure, combine milk, rum, and vanilla. Cook on High for 2 minutes, until hot but not boiling.

In a separate bowl, beat eggs and sugar together until frothy. Add to heated milk, and stir. Pour mixture into 4 custard cups. Place cups into the microwave in a circular pattern, allowing 1-inch space between them. Cook on *Medium* (50% power) for 6 to 8 minutes, or until firm, repositioning cups every 2 minutes for more even cooking. Chill. (Mixture may be put in freezer at this point for 20 minutes to speed cooling.)

To unmold, run a small knife around the outside edge of the custard. Invert a small serving plate on top of custard cup and quickly turn over. Carefully lift off custard cup from custard. Garnish the top of each custard with a glazed strawberry and mint leaf.

TIP
Custard is done when a knife inserted halfway between the center and edge comes out clean. Center appears soft but will set upon cooling. Overcooking will cause custard to be rubbery.

Mousse au Chocolat et au Moka

Chocolate-Mocha Mousse

Servings: 6   Preparation time: 10 to 15 minutes
                                      plus 1¼ hours
                                      to chill

¼ cup strong black coffee (espresso preferred)
2 tablespoons rum, brandy, or other liqueur
6 ounces semisweet chocolate pieces
¼ cup sugar
1 cup heavy cream

In a 4-cup glass measure or bowl, combine coffee, rum, and chocolate. Cook on High for 2 minutes, until chocolate is melted, stirring once during cooking. Stir at end of cooking to make smooth.

Add sugar and continue stirring until smooth and glossy. Cool. (Mixture may be put in freezer at this point for 15 minutes to speed cooling.)

In a small bowl, whip cream until thick. Fold into chocolate mixture. Spoon into individual stemmed glasses or demitasse cups. Chill for at least 1 hour before serving.

SERVING SUGGESTION
Serve each portion with a dollop of whipped cream, and grated chocolate or chocolate curls.

Mousse au Citron

Lemon Mousse

This lemon version is fresh, tangy, and light as sherbet. It's best served after a heavy meal.

Servings: 6   Preparation time: 30 to 35 minutes
                                    plus 2 hours to chill

⅓ cup strained lemon juice
1 teaspoon grated lemon rind
2 large eggs, separated
¾ cup granulated sugar
⅛ teaspoon cream of tartar
¾ cup heavy cream
2 tablespoons confectioners' sugar
Lemon rind, cut into thin strips, for garnish
Mint leaves for garnish, optional

In a 4-cup glass measure, combine lemon juice, grated rind, egg yolks and ¾ cup granulated sugar; beat with a spoon until well blended. Cook on High for 3 to 4 minutes, stirring every minute until frothy. Pour into a large mixing bowl to cool and thicken. (Mixture may be put in freezer at this point for 20 minutes to speed cooling.)

Drop egg whites into a deep bowl. Beat with electric mixer until frothy; add cream of tartar and beat until stiff peaks form. Fold whites into cooled lemon mixture.

Pour cream into a deep bowl. Beat with electric mixer until thickened. Add confectioners' sugar and beat until just blended. Fold into lemon mixture.

Spoon mousse into 6 dessert glasses and place in freezer for 2 hours until solid. (Mousse can be frozen at this point for 2 months if covered tightly.)

Garnish with lemon rind and fresh mint.

TIP

To get the greatest volume from egg whites, make sure that they are at room temperature, or 75°F. Use a deep bowl, but not aluminum, which will cause the eggs to turn color, or plastic, which may decrease volume.

Fraises Glacées

Glazed Strawberries

An attractive garnish for cakes or custards.

Quantity: 12 to 16   Preparation time: 5 Minutes

¼ cup currant jelly
½ pint whole strawberries, hulled, washed, and well dried

Place jelly in a 1-cup glass measure. Cook on High for 1 minute, or until jelly is melted. Allow to stand for 2 minutes to cool slightly so as not to cook the fruit.

Make sure that strawberries are thoroughly dried, then dip them, a few at a time, into the jelly. Remove with slotted spoon onto wax paper to cool. Use with mint leaves to garnish Pots de Crème.

Clafouti Limousin

Custard Tart with Cherries

Clafouti is a specialty of the Limousin, one of the ancient provinces of France. In this unusual dessert bright nuggets of whole, red cherries are baked into a pudding tart. But because cherries are so seasonal we've added Clafouti aux Pommes, a variation which can be made with apples all year round.

Servings: 6 to 8   Preparation time: 20 minutes plus
                                                     10 minutes to stand

1 tablespoon butter
1 pound cherries, washed and pitted
2 eggs, beaten
¼ cup sugar
¼ cup sour cream
1 tablespoon Triple Sec, or other orange-flavored liqueur

In a 9-inch microwave or glass pie plate, combine butter and cherries; cook on High for 1 minute.

Meanwhile, in a small bowl combine remaining ingredients; beat lightly with a wire whisk. Pour over cherries and butter. Cook on *Medium* (50% power) for 10 to 12 minutes or until custard just sets, rotating one quarter turn every 3 minutes.

Remove from oven and allow to stand for 10 minutes. Serve warm or chilled.

VARIATION
For Clafouti aux Pommes, increase butter to 2 tablespoons and cook in a 9-inch microwave or glass pie plate on High for 1 minute. Peel, core, and thinly slice 3 medium-size apples (Granny Smith or Rome). Arrange in an overlapping, circular pattern, in a single layer on top of the melted butter. Sprinkle with ¼ cup sugar and 1 tablespoon lemon juice. Cover loosely with wax paper and cook on High for 6 to 8 minutes, or until apples are tender.

In a small bowl combine egg, sour cream, and sugar in the same quantities as the basic recipe; add 1 tablespoon rum or vanilla extract and beat lightly. Pour over apples. Cook, uncovered, on *Medium* (50% power) for 8 to 10 minutes, or until custard just sets, rotating one quarter turn every 2 minutes.

Sprinkle top with ¼ teaspoon ground cinnamon. Remove from oven and allow to stand for 10 minutes. Serve warm or chilled.

TIP
During standing time, *clafouti* should be on a flat surface, not a cooling rack, to allow cooking to continue.

Noix Sucrées, Fruits Sucrés

Sugar-Glazed Nuts or Fruits

A nice addition to a dessert platter of fruit and cheese.

Quantity: about 2 cups   Preparation time: 15 minutes

1 cup sugar
¼ cup water
2 cups shelled nuts, orange segments, or whole strawberries, hulled, washed, and well dried

In a 1½-quart microwave casserole, combine sugar and water; mix well to dissolve sugar. Cook on High for 2 minutes; stir gently to redistribute heat. Cook for 6 to 8 minutes more, or until syrup is amber-colored and a spoonful becomes brittle when dropped into ice water. Stir syrup, once or twice, gently.

Working quickly, drop a few nuts or fruit into the syrup to coat, and remove individually with a fork onto buttered cookie sheet. The candy will begin to harden immediately.

TIPS
Stir sugar and water carefully as it cooks, without touching the sides of the dish. Too much stirring will cause it to crystallize.

Try to keep nuts and fruit individually coated or the finished product will be a candy brittle that needs to be broken apart.

Pouding au Moka

Mocha Pudding

Just like an old-fashioned steamed pudding but without the 3 to 4 hours it takes to bake in a water bath.

Servings: 6   Preparation time: 25 minutes

2 ounces German sweet chocolate
1 tablespoon butter
1 egg
¾ cup sugar
¾ cup prepared strong coffee
1 cup flour
1 teaspoon baking powder
Sauce au Rhum (Rum Sauce, page 149)

Cut a circle of wax paper to fit the bottom of a 4-cup French porcelain pudding mold, or 4-cup glass bowl; place paper inside mold.

In a 2-cup glass measure, place chocolate and butter. Cook on High for 1½ to 2 minutes, or until chocolate is melted. In a separate bowl, beat egg until frothy, blending in sugar gradually. Add melted chocolate and coffee, stirring to blend.

Sift flour and baking powder together; stir into chocolate mixture. Pour into prepared mold.

Cook on *Medium* (50% power) for 8 to 10 minutes, or until set, rotating one quarter turn every 2 minutes. Remove from oven and allow to stand on a flat surface for 5 minutes. Run a sharp knife around the edge of the mold and with a long-bladed metal spatula lift and invert onto a serving platter. Serve with Sauce au Rhum.

SERVING SUGGESTION

After spooning some of the Sauce au Rhum over the pudding, decorate with cream rosettes. In a small bowl, combine 1 cup heavy cream and 2 tablespoons confectioners' sugar; beat with . electric mixer until stiff. Fill a pastry bag fitted with a rosette tube and pipe small flowers on the bottom edge of the pudding.

TIPS

Pudding is done when a toothpick inserted in the center comes out clean. Moist areas on top will finish cooking during standing time. To test the moist areas for doneness underneath, touch the top lightly with fingertips. The moistness that sticks to your fingers will reveal dry cake below.

Allow the pudding to stand on a flat surface, not a cooling rack, to help contain the heat and continue the cooking.

Sauce au Rhum

Rum Sauce

Quantity: about 1 cup   Preparation time: 5 minutes

¼ cup sugar
1 tablespoon cornstarch
1 cup water
1 tablespoon grated lemon rind
4 tablespoons rum

In a 4-cup glass measure, combine sugar and cornstarch. Add water slowly and beat until smooth. Cook on High for 2 minutes. Beat well with whisk; cook for 1 minute more, or until thickened. Add lemon and rum; beat well. Serve warm over Pouding au Moka.

Ananas à la Crème

Cream-Filled Pineapples

Servings: 4   Preparation time: about 1 hour and 10
                         minutes, including
                         all recipes, plus 30
                         minutes to chill

Crème Pâtissière (Pastry Cream, page 136)
2 small ripe pineapples
2 tablespoons Triple Sec or other orange-flavored liqueur
4 butter-flavored cookies

Prepare Crème Pâtissière and chill.

With a sharp knife, cut pineapples lengthwise into halves, including the green leaves, which will remain attached. Trim any extra long leaves. Insert a grapefruit knife into the pineapple halves, approximately ½ inch from the edge. Cut around the edge as evenly as possible.

With a large spoon, remove pineapple flesh, leaving the ½-inch edge. Refrigerate the 4 shells. Remove core and cut remaining pineapple flesh into ½-inch cubes.

Place cubes in a microwave or glass pie plate. Add Triple Sec and cover loosely with wax paper. Cook on High for 4 minutes; stir. Cook for 2 to 4 minutes more. Cool pineapple in liquid. (Pineapple may be put into freezer at this point for 30 minutes to speed chilling.)

Add cooled Crème Pâtissière to pineapple flesh; stir gently to coat pineapple chunks. Spoon into chilled shells; replace in refrigerator to keep cold.

Place cookies in a plastic bag or between sheets of wax paper and crush with rolling pin; or use a food processor. Sprinkle crumbs on top of pineapple as a garnish.

SERVING SUGGESTION
Instead of crushed cookies, use chopped nuts, toasted coconut, macaroon crumbs, fresh raspberries, or mint leaves for garnish.

INDEX